OUTSPEAKS
A RHAPSODY

ALBERT SAIJO

BAMBOO RIDGE PRESS

1997

ISBN 0-910043-50-7

COPYRIGHT 1997 ALBERT SAIJO
ALL RIGHTS RESERVED BY THE AUTHOR. THIS BOOK, OR PARTS THEREOF, MAY NOT BE REPRODUCED IN ANY FORM WITHOUT PERMISSION.

ARTWORK FROM ORIGINAL MANUSCRIPTS
COVER AND BOOK DESIGN: SUSANNE YUU
TYPESETTING: WAYNE KAWAMOTO
PRINTED IN THE UNITED STATES.

PUBLISHED BY BAMBOO RIDGE PRESS.

BAMBOO RIDGE PRESS IS A NONPROFIT, TAX-EXEMPT ORGANIZATION FORMED TO FOSTER THE APPRECIATION, UNDERSTANDING, AND CREATION OF LITERARY, VISUAL, AUDIO-VISUAL, AND PERFORMING ARTS BY AND ABOUT HAWAII'S PEOPLE. YOUR TAX DEDUCTIBLE CONTRIBUTIONS ARE WELCOMED.

BAMBOO RIDGE IS SUPPORTED IN PART BY GRANTS FROM THE STATE FOUNDATION ON CULTURE AND THE ARTS (SFCA), CELEBRATING OVER THIRTY YEARS OF CULTURE AND THE ARTS IN HAWAI'I. THE SFCA IS FUNDED BY APPROPRIATIONS FROM THE HAWAI'I STATE LEGISLATURE AND BY GRANTS FROM THE NATIONAL ENDOWMENT FOR THE ARTS. BAMBOO RIDGE PRESS IS A MEMBER OF THE COUNCIL OF LITERARY MAGAZINES AND PRESSES (CLMP).

THIS PROJECT HAS BEEN SUPPORTED IN PART BY THE STATE FOUNDATION ON CULTURE AND THE ARTS, THE HAWAI'I COMMUNITY FOUNDATION, THE MCINERNY FOUNDATION, THE ATHERTON FAMILY FOUNDATION, AND AN ANONYMOUS DONOR.

THIS IS A SPECIAL ISSUE OF *BAMBOO RIDGE, A HAWAII WRITERS' JOURNAL*, ISSUE # 71, ISSN 0733-0308.

BAMBOO RIDGE IS PUBLISHED TWICE A YEAR. FOR SUBSCRIPTION INFORMATION, DIRECT MAIL ORDERS, OR A CATALOG OF OUR BOOKS, CALL OR WRITE:

BAMBOO RIDGE PRESS
P. O. BOX 61781
HONOLULU, HAWAII 96839-1781
(808) 626-1481

10 9 8 7 6 5 4 3 2 1   97 98 99 00 01 02 03 04 05 06

TO LAURA FOR EVERYTHING

ACKNOWLEDGMENTS

TO THE AT THE ELBOW ENCOURAGEMENT & PERSISTENCE OF CATHY SONG LOIS-ANN YAMANAKA JULIET KONO ERIC CHOCK DARRELL LUM WING TEK LUM NORA OKJA KELLER & BOONE & TAMARA MORRISON WRITERS ALL WHOSE WORK CAN STAND WITH ANYTHING IN THE LANGUAGE — TO THE VEHICLE *BAMBOO RIDGE* EVERYTHING A LIT RAG SHOULD BE

VAST BAMBOO GROVES ON MAUI
BETWEEN HAIKU & HANA BLOWN BY TRADES —
GREEN BILLOWING MASS OF BAMBOO
FROM GULCH UP TO RUNNING RIDGE

SOME OF THESE PIECES HAVE APPEARED PREVIOUSLY IN *BAMBOO RIDGE THE HAWAI'I WRITERS' QUARTERLY*

"SUMMER SOLSTICE" IS DEDICATED TO JERRY MARTIEN VOICE OF MANILA GEM OF ARCATA BAY

"IS LANGUAGE NECESSARY TO HUMAN EXISTENCE" AND "SAME HORIZON DIFF VIEW" FIRST APPEARED IN *BIG SKY MIND*

"LAST DAYS OF LEW WELCH" WAS WRITTEN FOR *HEY LEW*—EDITED BY MAGDA CREGG UPCOMING "FORM EMPTY" FOR MICHAEL WENGER WHOSE DROLL RIGHT ON SEARCH FOR THE AMERICAN KOAN 33 FINGERS INCLUDES THE HEART SUTRA

"KARMA LOLLIPOP" WAS AWARDED THE PUSHCART PRIZE XXI, 1997

I LIKE DRY LIGHT, & HARD CLOUDS,
HARD EXPRESSIONS, & HARD MANNERS.
                                    EMERSON

AS NONE TRAVELLING OVER KNOWN LANDS
CAN FIND OUT THE UNKNOWN,
SO FROM ALREADY ACQUIRED KNOWLEDGE
MAN COULD NOT ACQUIRE MORE:
THEREFORE AN UNIVERSAL POETIC GENIUS
EXISTS.
                                    BLAKE

CONTENTS

13	O MUSE
17	FIELD PREACHER
18	ANIMAL RHAPSODE
23	ANALGESIA
	LAND OF PAIN FREE
33	LET'S ALL BE POISONED TOGETHER
	WHO WANTS TO BE A LONE SURVIVOR
38	HOMO NERDUS
	INFO JUNKY
44	NATUREMART
46	NIGHT LIFE
	WAKING STATE ZOMBIE
50	SCIENCE
62	LUDDITE MANQUÉ
69	SYLLOGISM NO DOUBT
70	IS LANGUAGE NECESSARY TO HUMAN EXISTENCE
73	EARTH SLANGUAGE WITH ENGLISH ON IT
77	2 BOMBS

79	THE GULF WAR
106	TO IRISH HEROS
109	PROCRUSTES A RANT
114	KARMA LOLLIPOP
121	NO SHIT
122	I MUST BE APOSTATE FROM HUMAN
127	BODHISATTVA VOWS
128	NUMBNUT
129	MONKEY SEE MONKEY DO
130	NOBLE SAVAGE
131	COLUMBA LIVIA WITH PEOPLE IN URBAN SETTING
135	TREES
137	A BEAST FABLE
138	A KONA
146	SUMMER SOLSTICE
152	IF NOT CIVILIZATION THEN WHAT
157	FORM EMPTY READING THE HEART SUTRA AGAIN AFTER MANY YEARS
159	EYAT
163	COSMOVISION

167	MAMA DID YOU CALL
169	DEVA WORLD
170	SAME HORIZON DIFFERENT VIEW
171	TZADIKIM
172	TO ROBERT AITKEN GYŌUN-KEN ROSHI ON HIS RETIREMENT PĀLOLO ZEN CENTER O'AHU HAWAI'I WINTER SOLSTICE 1996
174	AGING A DEPLORATION
176	I RESIGN
178	HAPPY ZEROETH BIRTHDAY
179	LEW WELCH
191	ABOUT THE AUTHOR

O MUSE

YES I BELIEVE IN THE MUSE — LIPS PARTED TONGUE CURLED BUT MUTE — BLANK EYE-SHINE FOR EYES — O RADIOCARBONIC — HEART TO HEART TRANSMITTER — NOT JINXABLE — NEVER STINGY — BIOLUMINESCENT ONE — TELL ME THE UNIVERSE — GUIDE ME TO THE LAST PERIOD

THE CITY IS ESSENTIALLY A PSYCHOTIC CONDITION, TAKE IT HOW YOU WILL. WANT TO BEAR WITNESS, I W TO TELL YOU WHAT I SEE HAPPENIN BEFORE MY EYES, I CAN HARDLY ELIEVE WHAT I SEE HAPPENING BEFO MY EYES. ~~I WANT TO SPEAK~~ I WANT TO STAND IN A FI & PREACH. I WANT TO BE A FIELD PREACHER LIKE ~~I WANT TO SAY THE ANIMAL~~ OHN MUIR'S FATHER, I W O STAND IN A FIELD & PREACH I DON'T CARE IF ANYO HEARS ME. ~~LISTENING~~ I WANT T STAND UNDER AN OPEN SK IN A FIELD & I WANT T EXHORT OR LAMENT, I V ~~EJACULATE ENTHUSE~~ ~~EXPATRIATE BEWAIL ELEGIZE~~ OUTSPEAK I WANT TO LAY IT ON THICK. I WANT TO HOLD FORTH EXPOSTULATE I WAN TILL I'M SWEATING INCITE DECLAIM SERMONIZE TO RAVE ON. I WANT TO W UP A LATHER TIL FINALLY & GLO ~~TO ME~~

NON ME SPACE SOCIETY

THE BREADTH OF WHAT
WE ARE —

THE BEAUTY OF IT IS
I CAN GROW IT IN
MY OWN YARD — THAT ITS F

LOOK AT THE EVENING NEWSROAD THE
THE WORST THINGS HUMANS DO THEY DO
IN COMMUNITY

NO BOUNDARY

NATUREMART

HOW VERY PRESUMPTUOUS
OF US TO RESIGN FROM THE
REST OF NATURE & MAKE EARTH
ONE BIG NATURAL RESOURCE CALLING FOR DEVELOPME
VERY PRESUMPTUOUS OF US WITH NO PARLAY FOR OUR BENEFIT SOLELY WE'RE
TO TELL NATURE OK FROM NOW ON INSTAR
TREATING YOU LIKE
4 HOROLOGII — RATHER THAN
INSTAR DIVINE ANIMALIS WE'RE GOIN TO MESS
VERY PRESUMPTUOUS OF US DOWN
TO PLUNK OUR TRIP ON REST
A NATURE WIDE
OF EARTH WITHOUT A REFERENDUM
BIBLE SEZ WE GOT DOMINION BUDDHIST SAYS LUCKY YOU
NOT LESSER ANIMAL YOU TURN EARTH INTO INDUSTRIAL SITE OID
BORN HUMAN ITS OK HUINENS SEZ WHERE YOU THE DUST
EVEN THOREAU AT WALDEN WITH HIS I WANT T
MAKE THE EARTH SAY BEANS — RATHER THAT IS
THAN WHAT IT WAS SAYING BEFORE — HENRY
WHATS OUR TRIP — CONTROL — DOMINATION
ANTHROPOMORPHISE ALL OF NATURE — CAUGHT IN A TRULY PATHE
CREW LOOSE IN BRAINPAN MAKE EARTH
STORE SHELF

FIELD PREACHER

I WANT TO BEAR WITNESS — I WANT TO TELL WHAT I FEEL WHEN I SEE WHATS HAPPENING BEFORE MY EYES — I CAN HARDLY BELIEVE WHAT I SEE HAPPENING BEFORE MY EYES — I WANT TO STAND IN A FIELD & PREACH — I WANT TO BE A FIELD PREACHER LIKE JOHN MUIR'S FATHER — I WANT TO STAND UNDER AN OPEN SKY IN A FIELD & I WANT TO EXHORT & LAMENT ORACULATE ENTHUSE INVEIGH SCOLD RAIL STORM & RAGE RAGE ON WAIL & BEWAIL ELEGIZE & LYRICIZE INCITE DECLAIM EXPOSTULATE RAZZ SERMONIZE HARANGUE — I WANT TO OUTSPEAK — I WANT TO HOLD FORTH — RANT & RAVE — I WANT TO LAY IT ON THICK — I WANT TO MUCKRAKE — I WANT TO RHAPSODISE — I WANT TO PREACH TILL I'M SWEATING — I WANT TO WORK UP A LATHER TILL FINALLY I FALL BACK & THE SKY OPENS TO ME & GLORIOUS BEAUTY LIGHTS ON ME & I HEAR WHAT EVERY SON MUST HEAR & EVERY FATHER SAY — THIS IS MY BELOVED SON IN WHOM I AM WELL PLEASED

ANIMAL RHAPSODE

I LOOK UP RHAPSODY IN MY OED — AN EXULTED OR EXAGGERATEDLY ENTHUSIASTIC EXPRESSION OF SENTIMENT & FEELING — AN EFFUSION MARKED BY EXTRAVAGANCE OF IDEAS & EXPRESSION BUT WITHOUT CONNECTED THOT OR SOUND ARGUMENT — THIS DESCRIBES MY STYLE TO A T I THOT — AMONG OTHER MEANINGS OF THE WORD ARE — THE STRINGING TOGETHER OF POEMS — A MISCELLANEOUS COLLECTION — A CONFUSED MASS OF THINGS — A STRING OF WORDS SENTENCES TALES ETC — A LITERARY WORK CONSISTING OF MISCELLANEOUS OR DISCONNECTED PIECES — A WRITTEN COMPOSITION HAVING NO FIXED FORM OR PLAN — ALTOGETHER THIS APPEARS TO BE MY WORD I THOT — I THOT IF EVER I STRING TOGETHER A BOOK IT WILL BE A RHAPSODY — I TURNED THEN TO THE ROOT WORD RHAPSODE A COMPOUND OF THE GREEK WORDS FOR TO STITCH & SONG — THE QUOTATION SUPPORTING THE WORD IS FROM

COLERIDGE GRK POETS AS FOLLOWS — THESE RHAPSODES WERE INDIGENT PERSONS WHO GAINED THEIR LIVELIHOOD BY RECITING THE HOMERIC POETRY — I AM INDIGENT EVEN WHEN I HAVE MONEY — I LACK & AM IN CONSTANT WANT — I HAVE WRITTEN & RECITED POETRY — I AM A RHAPSODE — BUT MY TEXT IS NOT HOMER — MY TEXT IS THE WORLD I LIVE IN — RHAPSODIZE HAS THE MEANINGS TO UTTER RHAPSODY TO TALK RHAPSODICALLY TO EXULT TO CARRY ALOFT — I WANT TO RHAPSODIZE — BUT I WOULD NOT BE PUT INTO ANY LITERARY CATEGORY — I CAN HONESTLY SAY I HAVE NO LITERARY CONCERN — I AM AN ANIMAL IN A CAGE & I AM BARKING TO BE LET OUT — AS IT HAPPENS MY BARK IS RHAPSODIC

HELP US.

CRYIN IN YOUR BEER.

SNAPPING SUCKER SPRIGS OF
STOCK ROOTS

BURNING XMAS GREEN FIRE
MIC FIR
FOLIAGE VORACIOUSLY IN B??
ORANGE FLAME,

TO MAKE   ANALGESIA
        AMERICA   LAND OF THE PAIN FREE

PROPOSE A CRASH PROGR?
TO RELEASE SOCIETY FROM
PAIN BY THE YEAR 2000
I MEAN FAST, FAST RELIE?
                         BOTH PSYCH?
FROM PAIN OF EVERY KIND
     THE BOTTOM LINE
     EVEN ONTOLOGICAL PAIN OF UPHOLDING IMPROBABLE S?
                TOTAL RELIEF S?
VERYONE
              TWINGE
THERE IS NOT A
PAIN IN ANY HUMAN WORLD
IM TALKING ABOUT THE USE
EVERY KNOWN PAIN KILLER
FROM ASPIRIN TO ETORPHINE
                STRONGER THAN MORPHINE
5-10 TIMES   MASSIVE R?
              PAIN KILLING
        ???ER / SUBSTANCES.

~~THE SCIENTIST~~ SCIENCE ~~[illegible]~~

~~ART IS THE TREE OF LIFE~~
~~SCIENCE IS THE TREE OF DEATH~~
~~BLAKE~~

A RANT

WE MURDER TO DISSECT — WORDSWORTH

PLIABLE CREATURE WHO MEASURES — DOESN'T CARE WHAT YOU WANT MEASURED OR WHAT YOU'RE GOING TO DO WITH WHAT YOU GOT MEASURED — THAT'S CALLED ~~PLIABLE YET DOGMATIC~~ OBJECTIVITY — SCIENCE IS NOT ABOUT IMMEASURABLES LIKE FEELING DESIRE CHOICE IMAGINATION & THE BEAUTY OF BROAD DAYLIGHT ON EARTH — SCIENCE SQUELCHES AFFECTIVE PART OF NATURE — GOT TO — SCIENCE GETS NERVOUS CONFRONTED BY IMMEASURABLE — ALL THAT STUFF THAT'S NOT FALSIFIABLE. STILL THESE ARE THE GUYS WHO HAVE DELIVERED THE BENEFITS OF MODERN TECHNOLOGY BUT (AT THE SAME TIME) THEY ~~ALL~~ HAVE MADE US UNNATURALLY MARVELOUS IN ~~SO~~ WAYS THAT REALLY WEIGH ON THE REST OF EARTH. LIKE THE FACT EVERY MAJOR POLLUTANT WE SUFFER N[...]

ANALGESIA
LAND OF PAIN FREE

IT WAS ALMOST TIME FOR LUNCH.
PAIN IS HUMAN.
                            WALLACE STEVENS

I

I PROPOSE A CRASH PROGRAM TO RELIEVE HUMAN SOCIETY FROM ALL PAIN BY THE YEAR 2000 — I MEAN FAST FAST RELIEF FROM PAIN OF EVERY KIND BOTH MIND & BODY EVEN BASIC UNEASY ONTOLOGICAL PAIN OF UPHOLDING IMPROBABLE STATE CALLED LIFE — TOTAL RELIEF SO THERE'S NOT A TWINGE OF PAIN IN ANY HUMAN WORLDWIDE — I'M TALKING ABOUT MASSIVE RESEARCH INTO FINER & FINER PAINKILLING SUBSTANCES TILL WE HAVE ONE THAT WILL GIVE INSTANT PERMANENT RELIEF FROM ALL PAIN IN HUMAN LIFE — LETS TAKE THE BUCKS FROM HIGH ENERGY PHYSICS CANCER & CARDIOVASCULAR RESEARCH ALL THE BUCKS WE

COUGH UP TO SUPPORT MYTH OF CONTENDING NATIONSTATES HITECH AEROSPACE PROJECTS ETC ALL THE EARTH DESTROYING PROJECTS THAT GOT US KNEE DEEP IN SHIT EARTHWIDE & TURNED WORLD INTO A COMBO PLATE OF BIG MAC COKE FRIES WITH SIDE OF SUKIYAKI + 2 SCOOPS RICE & LETS TAKE THESE BUCKS TO FUND THE MOST AWESOME CRASH PROGRAM THE WORLD HAS EVER SEEN — LETS GET DOWN TO BASICS — LETS FORGET THOSE ENDLESS BULLSHIT PROJECTS WE'VE BEEN FRITTERING OUR TIME & MONEY AWAY ON & ADDRESS PROBLEM NUMERO UNO IN HUMAN LIFE — PAIN — THE TOTAL ELIMINATION OF PAIN BY THE END OF THE CENTURY — LETS MAKE NEUROENDOCRINOLOGY THE NEW GLAMOUR SCIENCE ALONG THE LINES OF THESE ARE THE GUYS WHO ARE GOING TO GIVE US FAST FAST RELIEF FROM PAIN FOR LIFE – HEADACHE TOOTHACHE PAIN IN THE NECK STUBBED TOE PAIN OF MILD OR SEVERE TRAUMA HURTFUL PSYCHIC STATES LOWER BACK PAIN ETC ALL THINGS OF THE PAST — HEY I GOT CANCER

& IT DONT HURT A BIT & I'M NOT EVEN WORRIED ABOUT IT — HEART ATTACK NO PROBLEM I JUST FELT A LITTLE BUMP & I FEEL JUST FINE NOW — AIDS JUST ANOTHER WAY TO GO — NO PAIN — I JUST LOST MY JOB & MY WIFE LEFT ME BUT THATS LIFE IT DONT HURT & I'M VERY OPTIMISTIC SOMETHING ELSE EQUALLY PAINLESS IS RIGHT AROUND THE CORNER — LIFE IS PAINFREE LARK — NO MATTER WHAT HAPPENS YOU MAY BE SURE OF ONE THING IT WONT HURT — WE CAN RELAX — RELAX DEEP — IT'S A MIRACLE — I AM ABSOLUTELY PAIN FREE THROUGH EVERY FIBER OF MY BEING — I MAY BE DYING BUT I FEEL GREAT — THESE NEUROENDOCRINOLOGY GUYS ARE SAINTS — GIVE EM ALL THE MONEY THEY WANT & THROW IN SOME NOBEL PRIZES FOR SURE

2

IF YOUR DEVOTION IS WHATS ON YOUR MIND MOST THEN OUR DEVOTION IS PAIN — PAIN IS WHAT HURTS BUT PAIN NEEDS NO DEFINITION IT IS UNIVERSALLY FELT & KNOWN — LIFE OF

BODYMIND COMBO HURTS PERIOD — ELIMINATE PAIN NOTHING HURTS — IS THERE LIFE BEYOND PAIN — ARE WE READY FOR PAIN FREE — WE WILL CHANGE — WE ARE SO ATTACHED TO HURTING WE THINK IT'S NATURAL BUT IS IT — WE ARE SO ATTACHED TO BEING PAINFULLY SICK & SAD — WE ARE SO CAREFUL TO BE SAFE FROM PAIN EVEN AS WE PAIN — WE FEAR PAIN & BUILD FORTRESSES AGAINST IT BUT PAIN ALWAYS MANAGES TO BREAK THRU EVERY DEFENSE & MAKE US HURT — WE GET NO RESPECT FROM NATURE PAINWISE — PAIN HAS BEEN OUR CONSTANT COMPANION SINCE BIRTH — I HURT THEREFORE I AM — & TO SAY A GOOD WORD FOR PAIN ISN'T IT ADVANTAGEOUS TO ORGANISM AS SIGNAL OF DISFUNCTION OR TRAUMA — BUT I ASK COULDNT NATURE HAVE COME UP WITH A SIGNAL THAT DIDN'T HURT — A GENTLE NUDGE SAY AS YOU WOULD NUDGE A LOVED ONE — HOWSOEVER — WITHOUT PAIN WON'T WE FEEL JUST EMPTY LIKE A DEFLATED BALLOON — A LARGE PART OF OUR HUMANITY IS A HERITAGE OF PAIN — PAIN IS NOT

ANCILLARY TO CIVILIZATION — CIVILIZATION IS SPECIFICALLY AN EXPRESSION OF PAIN — EVERY MAJOR HUMAN INSTITUTION DEPENDS ON PAIN BE IT GOVT CHURCH INDUSTRY OR COMMERCE — CIVILIZATION IS A MONUMENT TO PAIN — DO YOU REALIZE WHAT YOU'RE ASKING WHEN YOU PROPOSE PAIN FREE WORLD BY YEAR 2000 — YOU ARE ASKING US TO GIVE UP BEING WHO WE ARE — BUT WHO ARE WE — LETS FACE IT — AS WE ARE ARENT WE NOTHING MORE THAN ONE LONG EXERCISE IN PAIN MODULATION — IN SHORT YOU ARE ASKING US TO DIE TO OUR VERY SELVES — OUR VERY PAINFUL SELVES — WHAT PRICE PAIN FREE

3

WHERE TO FIND THE SUBSTANCE THAT WILL MAKE US PAIN FREE — FROM PERSONAL EXPERIENCE I KNOW THERE IS A SUBSTANCE IN MY BODY THAT IS CAPABLE OF SHUTTING OFF PAIN INSTANTANEOUSLY — IT HAS HAPPENED TO ME UNDER PHYSICAL TRAUMA — AN ENDOGENOUS OPIOID — ONE OF THE

ENDORPHINS — THAT GROUP OF PROTEINS OCCURRING NATURALLY IN BRAIN SOME WITH ANALGESIC POWERS FAR EXCEEDING MORPHINE — IT IS ONE OF THESE — ISOLATE IT — IT IS PART OF CODED RESPONSE OF BODYMIND TO ANY SITUATION THAT MIGHT LEAD TO DEATH — BODYMIND GOES ON HOLD — GOES INTO SHOCK OR BLACKOUT BOTH PAIN FREE LIMBOS IN WHICH TO ASSESS DAMAGE TO ITSELF & DECIDE TO GO FORWARD TO PAINLESS DEATH OR BACK TO HURTING LIFE — IF WE COULD FIND & ISOLATE THIS PAINKILLING SUBSTANCE & SOMEHOW SOFTEN IT SO IT BECOMES PAIN FREE IN LIFE RATHER THAN PAIN FREE IN LIMBO TOWARD DEATH — HERE WE SHOULD LOOK INTO THE NEUROBOTANY OF ANALGESIC & PSYCHOACTIVE PLANTS FOR HELP FOR INSTANCE MESCALINE IS EARTH LIFE ENHANCING — MESCALINE OR OTHER SIMILAR PLANT SUBSTANCE COMBINED WITH ENDORPHIN X COMBINED WITH SOME DE NOVO MOLECULAR CREATION AN ANALGESIC EUPHORIC SUBSTANCE SAY WITH THE POWER TO

PRESS & FIX PAIN FREE INTO BODYMIND PERMANENTLY — ONE PILL ONE TIME PERMANENT PAIN FREE — NO TOLERANCE DEPENDENCY FACTORS — NO DELETERIOUS PSYCHOPHYSICAL SIDE EFFECTS — JUST PAIN FREE — WE SIMPLY WANT OUR DAILY LIFE TO BE COMPLETELY PAIN FREE — IS IT TOO MUCH TO ASK TO BE AWAKE AMONGST THIS VARIED WORLD IN BROAD DAYLITE & BE COMPLETELY PAIN FREE

4

FORMERLY THE ONLY COMPLETELY PAIN FREE STATE WAS DEATH NOW THANX TO SCIENCE WE CAN BE COMPLETELY PAIN FREE IN LIFE — WE HAVE FOUND THE ENDORPHIN THAT IS RESPONSIBLE FOR THE STATE IN DEATH PROCESS WHERE ALL BECOMES ONE IN A TOTALLY NONJUDGEMENTAL SPACE IN A COMPLETELY PAIN FREE SETTING — IT CLICKS IN WHEN DYING ENDS & DEATH BEGINS — THE EYE OF COMPASSION OPENS AS PSYCHOLOGY DIES — THE

MYRIAD IDENTITIES OF THE WORLD MERGE INTO THE ONE GREAT IDENTITY — NOW WE HAVE THIS SPACE CAPTURED WITHIN A MOLECULE — BUT THIS SPACE IS TOO PURE TOO HIGH TOO BRILLIANT FOR OPERATING IN OUR DAILY LIFE SO IT MUST BE SOFTENED — PLANTS SOFTEN — A NEWLY DISCOVERED CACTUS INCREASES POWER OF FOCUS FAR & NEAR & MAKES OBJECTS SUPERCLEAR IN THEIR SHAPE & VOLUME — THE SPACE AROUND EVERYTHING TRANQUIL SOFT & LIGHT FILLED — BRINGS THE EARTH RIGHT UP CLOSE — BUT THIS COMBO OF ENDORPHIN & CACTUS IS TOO FASCINATING YOU STILL CANNOT MOVE FOR THE WORLD IN ALL ITS NOW SHARPLY DETAILED BEAUTY IS SPELL BINDING — YOU'RE ENTHRALLED & MOTIONLESS — THIS SPACE THO BEAUTIFUL WOULD BE EVOLUTIONARILY DISADVANTAGEOUS FOR YOU WOULD NOT DODGE THE FASCINATING BEAUTY OF THE ROCK FLYING TOWARD YOUR HEAD — IT WOULD OF COURSE BE A BEAUTIFUL PAINLESS DEATH BUT CONTRIBUTE NOTHING TO THE ADVANCE OF

CIVILIZATION — HERE A KICKER DE NOVO MOLECULE BREAKS SPELL OF BEAUTY WITH SOME GOOD OLD FASHIONED SELFISHNESS — NOT MUCH JUST SOME — ENUFF TO GIVE A SENSE OF A UNIFIED SELF IN A SURROUND OF OTHER SAME BUT DIFFERENT SELVES — ENUFF TO ENABLE YOU TO STEP OUT INTO BEAUTY OF DAY & MANEUVER WITHOUT BUMPING INTO ANY PART OF IT — IT'S A CASE OF JUST ENUFF CENTER OR TOO MUCH CENTER — ENUFF SO YOU CAN STEP OUT INTO THE WORLD AFFABLY WITH A CHEERY NOTE FOR EACH THING YOU PASS — YOU GREET EACH THING FEARLESSLY FOR YOU KNOW IT CAN'T HURT YOU — EGO IS PAIN SO NO PAIN NO EGO — WITH NO EGO PROPER THERE'S NOTHING TO PROTECT OR DEFEND — A TREMENDOUS SAVING OF PSYCHIC WEAR & TEAR — EVERYTHING THAT DEPENDS ON PAIN DISAPPEARS — HEALTH CARE INDUSTRY GOES BUST BECUZ NO ONE FEELS PAIN OR FEARS DEATH ANYMORE — NOTHING HURTS ANYMORE & IF IT DON'T HURT WHY MESS WITH IT — NO NEED CHURCH PRIESTS & COMPLICATED

RELIGIOUS DISCIPLINES — NOW ONE PILL DOES IT — THERE CAN'T BE RICH & POOR IF WHERE YOU'RE AT IS PAIN FREE — YOU'RE WHO YOU ARE DOING WHAT YOU'RE DOING & WHO YOU ARE & WHAT YOU'RE DOING IS PAIN FREE — YOU ARE BEYOND PAIN BASED GAIN LOSS LIKE DISLIKE PRAISE BLAME — YOU ARE PAIN FREE EQUANIMITY — EVERYONE HAS ABSOLUTE LIBERTY — YOU CAN MOVE IN ANY DIRECTION PAIN FREE & FEARLESS — IN DEEP RELAXATION OF NO FEAR THE EARTH STANDS OUT WITH ASTONISHING CLARITY & RAVISHING VACUITY — YOU HAVE NEVER SEEN IT BEFORE SUCH WAS YOUR PAIN — PAIN FREE INCREASES POWERS OF PERCEPTION & CURIOSITY — THE TOTALITY OF OUR LIFE SENSE RECEIVES A LIFT & HUMAN SOCIETY BECOMES A PLACE WHERE EVERY FACE YOU LOOK INTO SEZ PAIN FREE — YOU DON'T TRY TO HARM ANYONE — YOU KNOW IT'S IMPOSSIBLE — YOU DON'T TRY TO BENEFIT ANYONE — YOU KNOW IT'S IMPOSSIBLE FOR BEING PAIN FREE MEANS HAVING ALL YOU NEED — WE MUST HAVE IT — PAIN FREE BY THE YEAR 2000

LET'S ALL BE POISONED TOGETHER WHO WANTS TO BE A LONE SURVIVOR

AN ANECDOTAL DIATRIBE

LET'S ALL BE POISONED TOGETHER WHO WANTS TO BE A LONE SURVIVOR — WHO WANTS TO BE ALIVE IF EVERYONE ELSE IS DEAD — ASK ANY ADOLESCENT — THEY WILL TELL YOU THE WORLD HAS BEEN LATERED — SO WHY BE ORGANOVEGGIE — VEGGIES SCREAM TOO WHEN THEY'RE MURDERED — SHOULD PLANTS & ANIMALS BE ANESTHETIZED BEFORE BEING HARVESTED OR SHALL WE PROCEED IMMEDIATELY TO DE NOVO MOLECULAR SYNTHESIS OF FOOD — WHY NOT BRAISED BEEF SHORT RIBS WITH CARROTS & HERBS — CARDIAC DISFUNCTION IS THE PREFERRED FORM OF DEATH AMONG US ISN'T IT — AND FORGET HOW THE COW IS SLAUGHTERED — THOSE AGRIBIZ VEGGIES UNDER SPECIAL LIGHTS LOOK FLAWLESS MAYBE BECAUSE EVERY CREATURE THAT MIGHT HAVE

EATEN THEM WAS POISONED DEAD — FORGET IT — EAT — WE DESIRE TO BE FOOLED ABOUT RESIDUAL POISONS THAT WON'T WASH OFF BUT CANCER SMANCER WHAT'S THE DIFF SO LONG AS YOU'RE HEALTHY — YES LET'S EAT — OUR MARKETS ARE WELL STOCKED BRIGHT & CLEAN & SO SANITARY THERE ARE NOT EVEN TOILETS FOR THE CONSUMER — NO PISS & SHIT AROUND THE STORE THAT WAY — COME LET'S POISON OURSELVES TOGETHER WHO WANTS TO BE A LONE SURVIVOR — BUT THIS WATER IN THIS GLASS — ARE YOU MAD AT ME & ARE YOU OFFERING ME THIS WATER TO INSULT ME — THIS DIRTY WATER IN A CLEAN GLASS THAT SMELLS BAD & TASTES WORSE — DRINK IT — IT'S 100% SAFE — 9 OUT OF 10 DOCTORS RECOMMEND IT — THE NOXIOUS & TOXIC ADULTERANTS HAVE BEEN NEUTRALIZED BY OTHER LESS NOXIOUS & TOXIC ADULTERANTS — YOU DON'T WANT TO KNOW ABOUT IT — TRUST US — TAKE IT WITH A TWIST OF LIME & STIR WITH A SPRIG OF MINT — BE ORGANIC — WHAT HAVE WE DONE WITH THIS

ELEMENTAL JUICE THIS ACE MOLECULE OF LIFE — I WANT MY WATER TO TASTE LIKE WATER RUNNING OVER GRANITE WHEN I KNEEL DOWN TO DRINK IT IN HIGH MOUNTAINS — I WANT ANCIENT WATER OUT OF DEEP TAP — I WANT WATER OUT OF FAUCET TO POUR INTO GLASS LIKE SHORT FALL IN CLEAR BROOK THEN POND STILL IN GLASS TO CRYSTAL — AND I WANT THE WATER COLD SO IT MAKES GLASS FROST — BUT MY FRIEND MY FRIEND LET'S BE REALISTIC LET'S TAKE THE HORSE BY THE TAIL AND LOOK THE ISSUE SQUARELY IN THE FACE — AGREED THE WATER IS BARELY PALATABLE — BALANCE THAT AGAINST THE BENEFITS OF MODERN TECHNOLOGY — IN FACT I PROPOSE A TOAST A TOAST WITH THIS YOU MUST ADMIT ALMOST CLEAN WATER — HERE'S TO SCIENCE MAJORITY RULE & THE BENEFITS OF MODERN TECHNOLOGY — ONE TIME KNOCK IT BACK — THAT WASN'T TOO BAD WAS IT — MY FRIENDS LET'S POISON OURSELVES TOGETHER WHO WANTS TO BE A LONE SURVIVOR — AND WHY BE A CLEAN AIR

FREAK — WHY LIVE IN VIEW OF OCEAN WITH NOTHING HUMAN UPWIND ACROSS 3000 MILES OF WATER WITH WINDS ALWAYS DELIVERING AIR THAT IS LAMBENT CLEAR & MARINE IF CHERNOBYL GOES BLAM & WE FEEL LIKE PUKING & OUR HAIR FALLS OUT & WE FEEL SICK TO THE VERY MARROW OF OUR BONES WHILE AIR REMAINS LAMBENT CLEAR & MARINE — AH THIS TOO TOO PERISHABLE FRUIT DUMPED INTO DUMPSTER — YES LET'S POISON OURSELVES TOGETHER WHO WANTS TO BE A LONE SURVIVOR — MY FRIEND YOU MAY BE RIGHT BUT LET'S CONSIDER THE PROBLEM UNDER THE ASPECT OF ETERNITY — THE UNIVERSE CAN'T BE POLLUTED — SUCH POLLUTION AS WE GENERATE WILL BURN OFF ON THE LAST DAY — WE ARE ONLY FOULING OUR OWN NEST — EARTH — A STRICTLY LOCAL AFFAIR — WE ARE LIKE OUR COUSIN THE MOUNTAIN GORILLA WHO ALSO SHITS IN NEST — PUZZLING BUT NO BIG DEAL — THAT'S WHO WE ARE — SO LET'S POISON OURSELVES TOGETHER WHO WANTS TO BE A LONE SURVIVOR — AND

FINALLY WHO WANTS PURE UNPOISONED MENTALITY IF POISONED MENTALITY IS MAJORITY TAO — I EMBRACE THIS DESECRATION OF ANIMAL CALLED CIVILIZATION — HERMITS CAN'T BE POPULAR — AND WHO ON EARTH WANTS NOT TO SUFFER IF ON EARTH SUFFERING IS GENERAL AS GRAVITY — WHO NEEDS ENLIGHTENMENT THIS BASTARD DEATH THAT ONLY MAKES SUFFERING EXQUISITE — WHO WANTS TO BE GURU IF EVERYONE ELSE IS CHELA — LET'S BE IGNORANT TOGETHER — AS WE ARE — BORN FREE THEN POISONED THEN FROZEN — TOGETHER — LET'S BE POISONED TOGETHER WHO WANTS TO BE A LONE SURVIVOR

HOMO NERDUS
INFO JUNKY

1

INFO ADDICTION BASED ON VIEW OF LIFE AS A PROBLEM TO BE SOLVED — NOT LIVED — SOLVED — PART OF FUCKING GREEK IDEA THAT HUMAN MIND THINKING SYSTEMATICALLY CAN IMPOSE RATIONAL ORDER ON NATURE — JUST REQUIRES MORE INFO — INFO ADDICTION REQUIRES EVER HEAVIER DATA INTAKE — IF A LITTLE INFO GOT US THIS FAR THINK WHERE MORE INFO WILL GET US — TO SOME CYBER MUNDUS IMAGINALIS VIRTUALLY LIKE REAL BUT O NOT QUITE — ETERNAL JUNKY DREAM — I'M THIS HIGH CAN GET HIGHER — UP DOSAGE CONSTANTLY EVEN UNTO OVERDOSE

2

HOMO NERDUS SITS AT TERMINAL — H NERDUS PREFERS A ROOM WITHOUT A VIEW WITH SHADOWLESS LIGHT THAT STROBES FAINTLY &

HUMS — AMBIENT ELECTRONIC DRONE DROWNS OUT TINNITUS — SCENT CODED INFO PASSES THRU ROOM LIKE A PARADE OF DEODORANTS — INFO HOLOGRAPHICS PROJECTED INTO THIN AIR APPEAR & DISAPPEAR LIKE FATA MORGANA — HOMO NERDUS HAS PHONE PLUGS CHANNELING SEPARATE INFO INTO EACH EAR & IS TALKING INTO A BATTERY OF MIKES STATIONED AT HIS MOUTH WHILE VIEWING BIG SCREEN FOR BIG PICTURE & SMALLER SCREENS FOR SUBLIMINAL VIEWING OF PORNOINSTRUCTIONAL DATA IN WHICH DATA FUCK BRAIN MAKE BRAIN MOAN & COME — H NERDUS SUCKS IN FACTS LIKE GOOK SLURP NOODLES — LIKE VACUUM CLEANER SUCK UP DRY DUST — H NERDUS GET THIRSTY & PALMS SWEAT FROM ELECTROMAGNETIC RADIATION — H NERDUS TAKE VALIUM WITH GATORADE — HOMO NERDUS AMBIDEXTROUS CAN USE SIGN LANGUAGE WITH ONE HAND WHILE DOODLING ON FAX TO SHRINK WITH OTHER — 2 INDEX FINGERS NEVER FAR FROM BUTTON — H NERDUS HAS ANAL INSERT INFO SUPPOSITORY TO DELIVER

1ST CHAKRA INFO PUTS KUNDALINI IN REVERSE WITH AS YET UNTOLD CONSEQUENCES — STAY TUNED FOR MORE INFO ON THIS POTENTIALLY FASCINATING SUBJECT

3

HOMO NERDUS SITS AT TERMINAL — H NERDUS MOTIVATED — H NERDUS WANTS TO GET HIGH BUT DON'T KNOW HOW — BUT NOW H NERDUS FEELS TOP OF HEAD READY TO ERUPT WITH IDEA LIKE VOLCANO ERUPTS HOT LAVA — HOMO NERDUS SUDDENLY EXPLODES WITH ELECTRONIC EXCITEMENT — INSPIRATION LIGHT BULB GOES ON & IDEA BELL RINGS AS H NERDUS CONCEIVES ULTIMATE SURGICAL IMPLANT PROCEDURE IN WHICH ALL OF BRAIN DOWN TO STEM EXCISED & REPLACED BY A JILLION FLOATING POINTS PER NANOSECOND VIRUS FREE COMPUTER MINIATURIZED TO SIZE & SHAPE OF BRAIN IN A NICE BROWNISH PINK PROGRAMMED TO MAKE H NERDUS ACT LIKE YOU GUESSED IT A NORMAL BUT BETTER HUMAN BEING — A CROSS

DISCIPLINE CRASH PROJECT — FUND IT BY SAYING IT'S EITHER BRAIN IMPLANT OR GO EXTINCT — IT'S EITHER IMPLANT BRAIN SUPERIOR TO PRESENT OUT OF FASHION BRAIN OR BE WIPED OUT BY HIGHER TECH ALIENS FROM OUTER SPACE — WE CAN'T WAIT FOR EVOLUTION — YOU WANNA GO EXTINCT — NO ONE WANTS TO GO EXTINCT — ALRIGHT ALREADY — FIRST INSTRUCTION TO NEW BRAIN SEZ TAKE RECENTLY EXCISED OLD STYLE BRAIN WHICH WILL BE FOUND TO BE PRE SCRAMBLED & FRIED & EAT — SAVE PINEAL GLAND FOR LAST — CHOPPED COSTMARY GARNI OPTIONAL

4

SOME PEOPLE AINT GOING DOWN COMPUTER VISTA LANE — SOME PEOPLE THINK COMPUTERS BEND MIND TO MACHINE LOGIC GO TIC TAC FAST TO NOWHERE — ONE LONG BROWN STUDY — OR A SNORT OF HITECH COKE MAKE YOU GO BAZOOM BY THE NUMBERS — SOME PEOPLE THINK COMPUTERS ARE ULTIMATE INSTRUMENT

OF POLICE CONTROL BOTH INDIVIDUAL WITHIN SELF COMPUTER GENERATED NO FEELING POLICE COLD THOT & OUTER POLICE STATE COERCIVE SOCIAL CONTROL MADE FINE FORCING US TO DO WHAT WE DONT WANT TO DO TILL LIFE ITSELF BECOMES SOMETHING WE DONT WANT TO DO BUT ARE FORCED TO DO — COMPUTER PUTS ANIMAL SPIRIT TO BAD END — PUSHES HUMAN ENDEAVOR OUT OF SCALE — INHUMAN POWERS OF NUMERICAL COMPUTATION PRODUCE OUT OF SCALE OUT OF CONTROL SCIENCE GOVT MONEY COMBOS WHICH LOAD ON THE PEOPLE WITH LUNATIC MEGAPROJECTS THAT REWARD A COMPARATIVE FEW WHILE WASTING THE SPIRIT OF THE LAND & PEOPLE — LIKE THE VULGAR IDEA OF PUTTING A MAN ON THE MOON & LEAVING TRASH THERE — OR SPACE COLONIES — OR IDIOCIES OF HITECH WEAPONRY — LIKE HUMONGOUS UNDERGROUND ACCELERATORS THAT DONT WORK — LIKE WASTELAND MEDIA NETWORK SPREAD OVER EARTH & NEAR SPACE WITH ITS CONSTANT BAD NEWS MAKES EARTH

CRINGE — LIKE FORCING MILLIONS OF PEOPLE IN THE PRIME OF THEIR LIVES TO SIT AT TERMINAL BATHED IN ITS GHASTLY POISON LIGHT PUSHING NUMBERS THAT MAKE MONEY FOR OTHERS — TRILLIONS TAKEN FROM THE PEOPLE TO FUND THESE COMPUTER GENERATED MEGAMANIACAL PROJECTS WHILE BACK AT THE RANCH PEOPLE ARE TREATED LIKE SHIT ACROSS THE BOARD

NATUREMART

HOW VERY PRESUMPTUOUS OF US TO RESIGN UNILATERALLY FROM THE REST OF NATURE & MAKE EARTH SUN STARS ATMOSPHERE NEAR & DEEP SPACE INTO ONE BIG NATURAL RESOURCE CALLING FOR EARLY DEVELOPMENT IN HOMO SAPIENS' BEHALF SOLELY — HOW VERY PRESUMPTUOUS OF US WITH NO PARLEY TO TELL NATURE OK FROM NOW ON WE'RE TREATING YOU LIKE INSTAR HOROLOGII RATHER THAN INSTAR DIVINE ANIMALIS — KEPLER YOU BLEW IT — HOW VERY PRESUMPTUOUS OF US TO PLUNK OUR TRIP DOWN ON REST OF EARTH WITHOUT A NATUREWIDE REFERENDUM — BIBLE SEZ WE GOT DOMINION — BUDDHIST SAY LUCKY YOU BORN HUMAN & NOT A LESSER ANIMAL SO IT'S OK YOU TURN EARTH INTO INDUSTRIAL SITE & MORE ANGKOR WATS WHILE YOU'RE AT IT PLEASE — ANYWAY LIKE HUI NENG SEZ SINCE ALL IS VOID WHERE CAN THE DUST ALIGHT — EVEN THOREAU AT WALDEN WITH HIS I WANT TO MAKE THE

EARTH SAY BEANS — RATHER THAN WHAT IT WAS SAYING BEFORE HENRY — WE LOOK AT PANORAMIC SCENERY & SAY IT LOOKS LIKE A PAINTING IN A GALLERY — WHATS OUR TRIP — CONTROL — DOMINATION — CAUGHT IN A TRULY MONSTROUS INSTANCE OF PATHETIC FALLACY — ANTHROPOMORPHIZE EARTH — TURN ALL OF NATURE INTO STOREBOUGHT — SCREW LOOSE IN BRAIN PAN MAKE EARTH LOOK LIKE GOODS ON STORE SHELF

NIGHT LIFE
WAKING STATE ZOMBIE

SMOG OVER ARCTIC SO WE CAN ALTER NATURE'S PLAN TO HAVE DIURNALS ASLEEP SHORTLY AFTER DARK — WE DON'T HAVE THE ROUND EYES OR ECHOLOCATION OR ELECTROFEEL TO DO IT BUT WE WANT TO CONTINUE DAYLIGHT CONSCIOUSNESS INTO NIGHT WHEN PROPER DIURNAL MAMMALS ARE IN THE RADIANT BLACK OF DEEP SLEEP OR IN THE PRETERNATURAL DREAMSTATE — BOTH WHICH STATES WE CONTINUE TO BELIEVE IRRELEVANT TO WHAT IS CONSIDERED THE REAL ONE & ONLY LIFE ZONE FOR HUMAN — THE WAKING STATE — VISIBLE & INVISIBLE SMOKY RADIATIONS POISONOUS TO LIFE SPREAD OUT FROM SPOILED 4 CORNERS OF SW SO VEGAS & LA CAN MAINTAIN THEIR WAKING STATE ZOMBOID MODE THROUGH THE NIGHT — WE WON'T CLOSE DOWN THE WORLD WHEN IT GETS DARK — WE WANT TO GO INTO THE NIGHT WITH OUR DAYTIME WAKING STATE

CONSCIOUSNESS — WE WANT OUR NIGHTLIFE & WE'LL TURN EARTH TO CINDER FOR IT — WE'RE GOING TO MAINTAIN ZOMBOID WAKING STATE OVER EARTH 24 HOURS A DAY EVERY DAY INCLUDING HOLIDAYS — BUT NOW EARTH GETTING STRUNG OUT FROM LACK OF DEEP SLEEP — TOO MUCH LIGHT — TOO MUCH NOISE — EARTH EYES FEEL GRAINY — EARTH FEELING JANGLY GETTING IRRITABLE EVEN HAVE TANTRUM & THROW BACK GROSS MEDICAL GARBAGE ONTO BEACH — EARTH LOSING TREES LIKE MAN LOSING HAIR — EARTH BEGINNING TO HAVE BAD MORNINGS — EARTH COUGH HAWK UP SHIT — EARTH HAVING DRY HEAVES SO US CAN STAY UP — STAY UP PAST DARK WITH OUR MEANINGLESS DISPLAYS OF WAKING STATE RATIONAL BULLSHIT — TURN OFF THOSE FUCKING LIGHTS AND COME TURN IN

SCIENCE

WE MURDER TO DISSECT
                    WORDSWORTH

1

PLIABLE CREATURE WHO MEASURES — DOESN'T CARE WHAT YOU WANT MEASURED OR WHAT YOU'RE GOING TO DO WITH WHAT YOU GOT MEASURED — THAT'S CALLED OBJECTIVITY — PLIABLE YET DOGMATIC — SCIENCE IS NOT ABOUT IMMEASURABLES LIKE FEELING DESIRE CHOICE IMAGINATION & THE BEAUTY OF BROAD DAYLIGHT ON EARTH — SCIENCE SQUELCHES AFFECTIVE PART OF NATURE — GOT TO — SCIENCE GETS NERVOUS CONFRONTED BY IMMEASURABLE — ALL THAT STUFF THAT'S NOT FALSIFIABLE — STILL THESE ARE THE GUYS WHO HAVE DELIVERED THE BENEFITS OF MODERN TECHNOLOGY TO US BUT THEY HAVE AT THE SAME TIME MADE US UNNATURALLY MARVELOUS IN WAYS THAT REALLY WEIGH ON US & THE REST OF EARTH LIKE THE FACT EVERY MAJOR

POLLUTANT WE SUFFER NOW IS A PRODUCT OF SCIENCE — SMOG AT THE NORTH POLE — ANIMALS UP & DOWN FOOD CHAIN POISONED — WE GOT SCIENCE LIKE WE GET SICK — & AS FOR THOSE VAUNTED BENNIES OF MOD TECH NAME ME JUST ONE UNALLOYED BENEFIT OF MOD HITECH — JUST ONE — STILL YOU GOTTA SAY THEY'RE FUN GUYS WITH ENTERTAINMENT VALUE IF NOTHING ELSE — THINK OF THE GANG WHO MADE THE A-BOMB — HAVING TO NAME A-BOMB THEY CALL IT FAT-BOY — FUN BUNCH OF GUYS MAKE TOY GO BANG — PEOPLE DON'T EVEN HAVE TIME TO SCREAM WHEN IT HITS EM — AT GROUND ZERO VAPORIZED BODY LEAVES WHITE SHADOW — NOW THAT'S WIT — A WHITE SHADOW — AN ELEGANT CONCEIT — YOU WOULDN'T EXPECT LESS FROM THE BEST SCIENTIFIC MINDS OF THE TIME — & THE WAY THEY DID IT WAS SO CLASSY — THEY GOTTA MAKE THIS GODAWFUL THING & THEY AINT GOING TO LET ANYONE KNOW ABOUT IT — THEY GRAB SOME ENCHANTED LAND — THEY DON'T EVEN ASK AMERIND WHOSE LAND THEY GRAB IF IT'S OK — HOW CAN THEY — IT'S TOP

SECRET YOU UNDERSTAND — CLASSIFIED INFO — SECRET KNOWLEDGE ALWAYS KILLS — & GEE WHEN THEY BLASTED OFF TRINITY AT ALAMOGORDO THEY DIDN'T EVEN TELL AMERIND OR ANYONE ELSE FOR THAT MATTER ABOUT IT NOT EVEN A WORD LIKE HEY LOOK WE INVENTED THIS GODAWFUL THING ON YOUR PLACE & NOW WE GOTTA TEST IT & IT'S KINDA POISON BUT DON'T WORRY ABOUT IT — BETTER LIVING THRU SCIENCE — WHAT'S GOOD FOR SCIENCE IS GOOD FOR THE COUNTRY — IN THIS INSTANCE SQUASH JAP — THESE FUCKERS EVEN HAD A PLAN TO ASSASSINATE HEISENBERG JUST IN CASE HE WAS WORKING ON AN A-BOMB FOR GERMANY — HEISENBERG THE PURE MIND GAVE MODERN WORLD ONE OF THE MORE ELEGANT STATEMENTS FROM SCIENCE IN HIS UNCERTAINTY PRINCIPLE — OFF THE KRAUT — YOU GOTTA SAY THESE FUCKERS PLAY HARDBALL — THIS FRATHOUSE OF JOCULAR MURDERERS — THIS CLUB OF MALE NERDS — I RECALL THAT CLASSIC PHOTO TAKEN AT ALAMOGORDO JUST AFTER 1ST A-BOMB BLAST ON EARTH — ROBERT OPPENHEIMER &

GENERAL LESLIE GROVES LOOKING LIKE TWO BOYS IN ADULT BODIES STANDING ON THE PARCHED & CRACKED EARTH AT GROUND ZERO THEIR FEET CLAD IN NEAT WHITE PROTECTIVE OVERSHOES TO KEEP OFF THE NASTY RADIATION SMILING AT EACH OTHER POSITIVELY NUPTIALLY BEFORE A MESS OF TWISTED REBAR POKING OUT OF A PILE OF CRUMBLED CONCRETE — HERE IS THE FORMAL WEDDING OF SCIENCE & THE MILITARY INDUSTRIAL COMPLEX — THE DEADLIEST FORCE ON EARTH TODAY — LETS PULL THE PLUG ON THESE MOTHERFUCKERS — & WHEN THEY AREN'T INVENTING NEW WAYS TO TERMINATE CONSPECIFICS IN LARGISH NUMBERS THEY ARE BUSY INVENTING WAYS TO KILL OUR PEST ANIMALS & UNDESIRABLE VEGETATION — FLASH — SCIENCE DISCOVERS DOOMRAY — IT SIMPLY KILLS EVERYTHING IT TOUCHES — KOAN — WHAT IS A DEAD RAT'S ASS WORTH — A LEADING QUESTION — IS IT TIME TO SET UP AN INTERNATIONAL TRIBUNAL TO BRING TO JUSTICE THOSE SCIENTISTS WHO ARE RESPONSIBLE FOR THE KILLING OF MILLIONS OF

THEIR FELLOW HUMANS CHILDREN WOMEN & MEN IN OUR TIME — THOSE SCIENTISTS RESPONSIBLE FOR DESTRUCTION OF BIOME ON A SCALE TO DWARF NATURAL CATASTROPHIC EVENTS — AND LETS DISALLOW THE DEFENSE THAT WE JUST THINK UP THE BOMBS WE DON'T DROP EM — LETS MAKE THE GUYS AT THEIR DESKS DESIGNING THESE HORRORS TAKE RESPONSIBILITY FOR THEM — DISALLOW THE DEFENSE THAT SCIENCE IS A CORPORATE BODY OF KNOWLEDGE & THERE IS NO PERSONAL RESPONSIBILITY EXCEPT WHEN IT'S TIME TO HAND OUT THE NOBEL PRIZES — ARE YOU OR ARE YOU NOT ONE OF THE GROUP OF SCIENTISTS THAT DESIGNED THE A-BOMB THAT MURDERED OVER 200,000 HUMANS WITH JUST 2 BOMBS — IF YOU ARE THEN YOU ARE GUILTY OF MASS MURDER & YOU GOTTA PAY THE PRICE — NO ONE FORCED YOU TO DESIGN THESE HORRORS — YOU DID IT OF YOUR OWN FREE WILL WITH NO EXTENUATING CIRCUMSTANCES — WHAT WOULD BE A SUITABLE PUNISHMENT — WHO KNOWS — CERTAINLY EXECUTION WOULD BE TOO LENIENT — & WHAT

WOULD BE A SUITABLE PUNISHMENT FOR A CORPORATE BODY OF KNOWLEDGE THAT WILL GO TO OUR MOON & LEAVE TRASH ON IT — LET US HAVE AN ANTI-LITTER LAW ESPECIALLY FOR SCIENCE — MEANTIME BACK AT EL RANCHO ENCHANTED LAND IT HAS BEEN CLOSED & TURNED INTO A NUCLEAR WASTE DUMP & ART CENTER — WHY DOES EXACTNESS CONSISTENCY PREDICTABILITY FALSIFIABILITY RATIONALITY LEAD TO POLLUTION FEAR & MASSIVE PARANOIA & MAKE EARTH AN UNSAFE PLACE TO BE — LIKE SOME ROMAN SAID I FEAR NO MADNESS LIKE RATIONAL MADNESS

2

NATURE & LIFE ARE NOT WHAT SCIENCE SEZ THEY ARE — SCIENCE IS MERELY A WAY OF TALKING ABOUT NATURE & LIFE — IT IS A DREAM OF SEQUENCE — SCIENCE SEES NATURE AS MECHANICAL CLOCKWORK — KEPLER THIS CENTRAL FIGURE IN MODERN SCIENCE PUT IT IN A NUTSHELL WHEN HE SAID I USED TO THINK THE

UNIVERSE WAS INSTAR DIVINE ANIMALIS BUT NOW I SEE IT IS INSTAR HOROLOGII — THE METHOD IS SYSTEMATIC ABSTRACTION BY MEASUREMENT OF A SOMETHING OUT THERE BY A SOMETHING IN HERE — LIKE EINSTEIN SAID THE BELIEF IN AN EXTERNAL WORLD INDEPENDENT OF THE PERCIPIENT SUBJECT IS THE FOUNDATION OF ALL SCIENCE — THIS DISCONNECTION OF SOUL & PHENOMENA IS THE SICKNESS OF ALBION BLAKE SPEAKS OF — SCIENCE LOOKS & IT SEES BUT IT DOES NOT TRULY RECOGNIZE THE WORLD BECUZ IT HAS PUT ITS OWN NAME & CATEGORY ON ALL EVENTS & IT IS LOST IN THIS WORLD OF ITS OWN DEVISING — SO SCIENCE IS BLIND DUMB & DEAF TO DAME NATURE THAT'S WHY IT CAN DO WHAT IT DOES TO HER LIKE FINGER FUCK HER — UNCONNECTED SCIENCE ZOMBIE WHO SEES NATURE AS A CLOCKWORK COLLECTS DATA & EXTRAPOLATING FROM DATA MAKES WORKING MODELS & THEORIES — FUDGE MODEL SMOOTH OUT DATA FOR GOOD FIT — BUT NO COLLECTION OF DATA CAN COME ANYWHERE NEAR DUPLICATING OR MODELLING THE EVENT IT'S

TRYING TO DESCRIBE — THE MODEL OR THEORY IS ALWAYS FAR SHORT OF ORIGINAL NATURE BUT IT DOES GIVE SCIENCE JUST ENOUGH OF A PICTURE OF NATURE SO IT CAN USE NATURE — BUT TO BE ABLE TO USE SOMETHING IS NOT NECESSARILY TO KNOW IT — UNIVERSE HAS NO SIZE IT HAS NO EXTENSION NOR IS IT A POINT — UNIVERSE DOESN'T MIND HOW IT'S DESCRIBED — IT WILL ACCEPT EVERY MEASURE & DEFINITION OF ITSELF & IF PRESSED WILLINGLY MANIFEST THAT DEFINITION AS SQUEEZED DOLL SAYS MAMA — SCIENCE IS A TRIP LIKE ANY OTHER — IT'S THE SYSTEMATIC APPLICATION OF SOME BASIC ASSUMPTIONS LIKE EINSTEIN'S QUOTED EARLIER OVER AN EVER BROADENING DATA BASE — UNIVERSE IS AN ENDLESS STORE OF DATA — BUT DATA & THEORY LEAVE YOU WITH JUST DATA & THEORY — HOWLING EMPTY DESOLATE DATA & THEORY — SCIENCE WANTS WORLD FINITE PREDICTABLE & ANOMALY FREE — INFINITY MAKES SCIENCE NERVOUS BECUZ INFINITY IS NOT FALSIFIABLE — YOU CAN GET NEITHER IN NOR OUT OF IT — UNABLE TO FACE INFINITY SCIENCE COMES

UP WITH A CREATION MYTH THAT IS OUT OF A COMIC STRIP SURELY — THE UNIVERSE STARTED WITH SOME ORIGINAL SHIT EXPLODING WITH A BIG BANG IN A TIME LIKE SPACE & THE FORCE OF INITIAL EXPLOSION IS SCATTERING BITS OF THIS SHIT OUTWARD EVER OUTWARD WHILE LUCKY FOR US ON ONE PIECE OF SHIT BY THE ANTHROPIC COSMOLOGICAL PRINCIPLE OPERATIVE IN THE UNIVERSE FAVORING THE DEVELOPMENT OF LIFE & INTELLIGENCE YOU & I APPEAR BY PURELY CHEMICAL REACTION + EVOLUTION TO THINK UP A UNIVERSE THAT STARTS WITH ONE BIG HELLUVA BANG — HOLD IT RIGHT THERE — IS THE PHONOGRAPH RECORD BROKEN OR IS THIS A CASE OF SELF AUTHENTICATING CIRCULAR LOGIC — WHERE DID THE ORIGINAL SHIT THAT EXPLODES COME FROM — WHAT WENT BANG — WHERE DID THE TIME LIKE SPACE THIS HAPPENS IN COME FROM — CAN A UNIVERSE REALLY START — AND THIS UNIVERSE YOU'RE TALKING ABOUT — IS THERE SUCH AN ANIMAL — & IF SO IN WHAT ZOO OF YOUR IMAGINATION DOES IT EXIST — COME ON GUYS YOU

CAN DO BETTER — SCIENCE GOT TO GET STONED & COME UP WITH A WAY OF TALKING ABOUT NATURE LESS SIMPLISTIC DOGMATIC CLEVER UTILITARIAN CRASS & ARROGANT THAN ITS PRESENT MECHANICO WHIZZO BLATHER — A WAY OF BEING LESS HEAVY & VULGAR IN THEORY PRACTICE & APPLICATION

3

THE CHURCH OF NEW SCIENCE

ZERO TO THE BONE
EMILY DICKENSON

TIME — NOON — AUTUMN IN THE YEAR ZERO OF FRESH TIME

PLACE — LHASA — CAPITOL OF NEW SCIENCE — ALPINE PLATEAU WITH MONADNOCKS SURROUNDED BY PEAKS COVERED IN PERPETUAL SNOW & A SKY THAT IS A PURITY OF BLUE PRESSING DOWNWARD

SCENE — CHARTERHOUSE OF LHASA — PORTALA CONVENTION CENTER — A LONG LOW HALL WITH A FLAT GLASS ROOF THAT CAN OPEN BY FOLDING — ROOF HELD UP BY A FOREST OF POSTS SUPPORTING BRANCHY TRESTLEWORK PAINTED IN ANCIENT TIBETAN STYLE — LIGHT OF AUTUMN DAY AT NOON CASCADES DOWNWARD OVER SPACE OF HALL — A CONVOCATION HONORING NOVITIATES IN PROGRESS — POPE OF SCIENCE STEPS TO PODIUM — HE IS HOMUNCULAR — ALL HUMANS ARE NOW HOMUNCULAR FROM EXCESSIVE TECHNOLOGY OF ANCESTORS — SMALL & DARK — THE POPE IS ANCIENT YET TO BE IN HIS PRESENCE IS TO BE IN THE PRESENCE OF PUER AETERNUS — HIS FACE SHINES WITH LUMEN NATURALE BRIGHT OPEN FRANK — HE HAS NO BOUNDARY — HE IS TRANSPARENT AS CRYSTAL —

HE SEZ WELCOME TO NEW SCIENCE — THE CHURCH OF NEW SCIENCE — OUR SIMPLE DOGMA EARTH NATURE IS A BREATHING ANIMAL — WE BELIEVE

SCIENCE IS FOR FITTING HUMAN TO EARTH NATURE ACCURATELY — WE SEE NATURE AS PART OF NATURE REMEMBERING WE ARE NOT IN TIME LIKE SPACE WE ARE TIME LIKE SPACE — WE BELIEVE WE MUST KNOW WHO WE ARE BEFORE WE CAN KNOW NATURE — WE ARE NO LONGER SCIENCE UTILITARIAN BUT SCIENCE AS WITNESS OF EARTH NATURE — IN EACH CHARTERHOUSE OF NEW SCIENCE WE MEDITATE THE WELFARE OF NATURE CONSTANTLY — WE DECRY THE NETHER PERIOD OF SCIENCE WHEN IT BECAME MAMMONIC & COVERED EARTH WITH POISON & MISERY & THE LAST GREAT DISASTER — THIS CORPORATE MONSTER OF MEASURED MANIPULATION EXPLOITATION DOMINATION OVERKILL WHO WOULD TORTURE EARTH & ITS BEINGS FOR KNOWLEDGE BENEFICIAL TO ITSELF SOLELY — WHEN IT DIED EARTH CHEERED & RIGHTLY — BUT WE WILL NOT PISS ON THEIR ASHES FOR THEY WERE HUMAN AS WE ARE HUMAN — THEIR THEORIES HAVE GONE BACK TO THAT COLD PLACE WHERE TOTEMS OF THEORY RESIDE — WE STILL KEEP TO THE ORIGINAL ORPHIC MEANING

OF THEORY PASSIONATE SYMPATHETIC CONTEMPLATION & ECSTATIC REVELATION — WE NOW RECOGNIZE SCIENCE IS BEST PRACTICED IN A SETTING THAT IS MONASTIC & COMBINES THE EREMITIC & THE CENOBITIC — THE VOW TO DISCOVER THE HEART OF NATURE IS SOLITARY — TO DISCARD MEMORY & DIE TO THEORY IS SOLITARY — YOU CANNOT PRACTICE OUR SCIENCE UNLESS YOU ARE DEAD TO THEORY — O NOVITIATES YOU HAVE TAKEN YOUR VOW OF PERSONAL POVERTY & THE JOINT VOW TO KEEP OUR CHURCH EVER MORE SPARE POOR & MINIMUM — YOU GO TO YOUR CAVE — YOU HAVE YOUR MAT YOU HAVE YOUR BOWL — YOU WILL GROW THIN & PARSIMONIOUS — WHEN YOU ARE DEAD YOU WILL STEP OUT OF YOUR CAVE & FALL TO YOUR KNEES FOR YOU SEE EVERY EVENT IN NATURE IS HOLY & ETERNAL — WORSHIP IS THE NATURAL RESPONSE — YOU STAND UP — HOLY DATA FLOWS OVER & THRU YOU & YOU DO NOT COLLECT IT — YOU ARE IT — YOU STEP LIGHT ON THE CRYPTOSPHERE — YOU ARE READY TO BECOME CENOBITIC & JOIN IN THE VOCATION OF OUR

CHURCH — OUR SCIENCE IS NOT BASED ON NUMBER FOR WE SAW NUMBER & COUNTING ALWAYS RAN TO MEGALOMANIA & MAYHEM — WE NO LONGER COUNT — WE HAVE REPLACED NUMBER WITH YANTRA OUR PICTOGRAPH NOTATION MULTIPHASAL & MULTIDIMENSIONAL — WE HAVE DISCOVERED THE SET OF RADICAL YANTRAS THAT FORM THE BASIC MANDALA OF CREATION — A QUIET STILL FORMULATION THAT EXPLAINS EVERYTHING — TO LOOK INTO THE DESIGN OF ANY YANTRA GIVES ONE THE NAME DESCRIPTION & FEELY PRESENCE OF ITS EVENT BY CREATIVE VISUALIZATION PROJECTION BEING — EACH YANTRA SOUNDS ITS MANTRA — THE MANDALA OF CREATION GIVES OFF THE SOUND OF EVERYTHING WE NEED TO SAY AS HUMAN — MANTRA & YANTRA TOGETHER TRANSLATE INTO MUDRA THE GESTURE OF OUR BLOOD & FLESH LIVES — WE ARE NOT INTERESTED IN HOW THINGS WORK — RAPTURE IS THE GOAL OF SCIENCE

LUDDITE MANQUÉ

TO LUREENA GODDESS OF COMMODITY MOBILITY & CONVENIENCE

O SMART & BEAUTIFUL — O LUSCIOUS FULFILLMENT — O PROTEAN DESIRE — O EVER SHINY — KEEP ME IN COMMODITY FROM YOUR ENDLESS LARGESS O THOU RICHNESS — GET ME WHERE I'M GOIN FAST FAST WITHOUT PERSPIRATION — MAKE THINGS EZ — KEEP ME EVER NEW & IN MOTION

I WOULD GO OUT & SMASH MACHINERY BUT FOR THE FUTILITY OF ONE MAN AGAINST THE WORLD — BESIDES I'M A MAN OF THIS WORLD & I'M HOOKED ON MACHINERY — JUST LIKE YOU — I WORSHIP LUREENA — SHE'S AN HONEST GODDESS — SHE DELIVERS — I WOULDN'T DIE FOR JESUS OR BUDDHA BUT I WOULD DIE FOR LUREENA — I OFFER MY LIFE TO HER EACH TIME I GET IN MY CAR — I AM EVER OPEN TO

HEADONCOLLISION & SACRIFICIAL DEATH AT 60 MPH FOR LOVE & DEVOTION TO LUREENA — SHE HAS REDUCED DESIRE-FULFILLMENT GAP TO ALMOST NOTHING — WITHOUT A DOUBT SHE'S MADE LIFE EZ & ELIMINATED SWEAT FACTOR ACROSS THE BOARD — SHE'S A REGULAR CORNUCOPIA OF COMMODITY CONVENIENCE & MOBILITY — TO ME SHE'S PREMIER CUNT AMONG DIVINES — SHE'S BEAUTIFUL — SHE'S DESIRABLE — I'D LIKE TO FUCK HER — LIKE I SAY I'D DIE FOR HER & YOU CAN'T BE MORE DEVOTED THAN THAT — STILL I'M A LUDDITE BECUZ I SEE WHAT MACHINES & MACHINE MENTALITY HAVE DONE TO ANIMAL ME & MY EARTH — BUT PERFORCE I'M A LUDDITE MANQUÉ — THE MACHINE IS NOW BIGGER THAN ANY MONKEY WRENCH THROWN INTO ITS MAW — THEY GOT MACHINES NOW THAT DIGEST MONKEY WRENCHES — I LOOK AROUND & SEE THE MACHINE EATING UP EVERYTHING — I SEE IT HAS MADE EARTH INTO AN INDUSTRIAL SITE & WASTE DUMP — MACHINE IS DEFINITELY ON A LONG ROLL WORLDWIDE —

BUT MACHINE HAS A FLAW — HARD AS IT IS IT IS BUILT OF SOMETHING NONMECHANICAL & SOFT FROM THE INVISIBLE REALM — DESIRE — TURN OFF DESIRE & MACHINE COLLAPSES — OUR DEVOTION TO LUREENA IS PAID IN DESIRE THAT NEVER GIVES OUT — BROAD INFINITE DESIRE SUFFERING NOVELTY IN A TIME LIKE SPACE — BUT DESIRE IN TURN HAS A FLAW — IT CAN BE TURNED OFF ALSO — THIS IS ONE OF THE DEEPEST FACTS OF NATURE HUMANS HAVE COME UP WITH — DESIRE CAN BE TURNED OFF NONMECHANICALLY — INVISIBLE SWITCH — ON — OFF — I BEEN TURNING THIS SWITCH OFF MORE & MORE LATELY — THERE MAY BE RELAPSES & BINGES BUT THE GENERAL TREND FOR ME HAS BEEN TOWARD OFF RATHER THAN ON — I'M NOT REJECTING LUREENA — I AM REFINING MY WORSHIP OF LUREENA & I THINK SHE APPRECIATES THAT — WHAT I MEAN IS I'M GETTING MINIMUM — ALL I WANT IS TO KEEP SOME TRUE SENSE OF AN ANIMAL UP ON ITS HIND LEGS ON A PLANET IN DEEP OUTER SPACE & IF A

MACHINE WILL HELP ME I WANT THE SMALLEST MACHINE LUREENA MAKES — MY MAIN VOTIVE TO LUREENA IS MY CAR OF COURSE — IT IS THE MAIN VEHICLE OF MY DESIRE — MY CAR TO ME IS AS WINGS ARE TO A BIRD — I'M SURE IT'S THE SAME WITH YOU — YET I KNOW BEHIND MY CAR ARE RANK ON RANK OF HUMANS WORKING UNDER CONDITIONS NO ANIMAL SHOULD BE MADE TO BEAR — RANK ON RANK OF HUMANS UNDER INVIDIOUS FORMS OF POLITY FORCED TO GIVE UP THE PRIME OF THEIR LIFE TO ASSEMBLY LINE REGIMENTATION MAKING THE TOYS OF OUR DESIRE — I KNOW BOTH SMOKESTACK & KLEEN INDUSTRY BUST UP EARTH & BELCH POLLUTION — I HEAR EARTH CRYING YOU'RE HURTING ME — I WANT TO WIPE OUT THE ARBITRARY SOCIAL SYSTEM THAT SAYS ALL THIS IS OK — THEN COMES LUREENA — SHE IS SOOO BEAUTIFUL I FORGET EVERYTHING ELSE & I WOULD EVEN CRAWL TO HER IF THAT WAS THE ONLY WAY I COULD GET CLOSE TO THAT LUSCIOUSNESS — I GOTTA ADMIT LUREENA GOT ME BY THE BALLS —

I MEAN I LOVE MY CAR AT THE SAME TIME I WANT TO TAKE SLEDGEHAMMER TO CAR FOR SPOILING EARTH — BUT I COP OUT & I DON'T SEEM TO MIND IT — SO LIKE I SAY I'M A LUDDITE MANQUÉ — I LOOK AROUND EARTH & FEEL UNEASY AS YOU DO WHEN YOU FEEL YOUR CAR IS USING MORE OIL THAN IT SHOULD OR RIGHT FRONT HAS SLOW LEAK — I MUST GET TO LUREENA CHURCH MORE OFTEN — LIKE EMERSON SAID THINGS ARE IN THE SADDLE & THEY RIDE MANKIND

IS LANGUAGE NECESSARY
TO HUMAN EXISTENC[E]

[LA]NGUAGE IS A BODY OF SUFFERING
WHEN YOU TAKE UP LANGUA[GE]
[YOU] TAKE UP THE SUFFERI[NG] CONTAINED IN THE LANG[UAGE]
[WOR]DS [ARE] IN[VENTED] THE CONSTANT COMPANION OF OUR MEN[TAL]
TALKING ABOUT THE [CONSCIOUS]
WEIGHS ON [LIKE PROBLEMS THAT] BODY O[F]
[WE]IGHT LANGUAGE MAKES S[OMETHING] MOVING &
[THE] WAY IT TAKES SOMETHING BUT LANGUAGE CAN TURN AROUND IN THE LANGUAGE DREA[M]
MAKE IT STILL, A MENTAL ARTIFACT A [OBVIOUSLY]
TO EVERY MEANING [MATERIAL]
[S]O WE ARE EVERYTHING WE CAN SAY. [THIS IS HEAVY.] THAT SOMETHING SO ABSTRACT
PRESSES IN BUT CONSTANT PRESSURE
[I]S SO POWERFUL (ESPECIALLY MEASURED WORDS) ON MENTALITY,
[MEASURED] WORDS, EACH OF US STARK RAVING IN OUR OWN WAY
FINALLY DRIVES MAD I[F]
[O]NE COULD SCREAM OUT O[UR]
INNER VOICE THEN AS IN TOURETTE'S SYNDROME.
SPOKEN WE'D ALL GET TO[SEE]
[A]N DA M[ANY] PUBLIC PEOPLE W[HO]
[HA]S NOT BEEN TRAPPED IN A
[WO]RD PRISON? WHO DOES NOT
[KN]OW SPIRALING WORD [ART]
[A]RT IS O? YET, FOR BETTER OR WORSE, WE MAKE LANGU[AGE]
[NUM]BER ONE TOOL OF MENTALITY.
[PERHAPS] THERE IS NO

BETTER HERE? MAYBE ~~~~, ALL WORS
TELL ME A TRUE BENEFIT
DERIVING FROM LANGUAGE.
CAN A GOOD COME OF IT?
PURVEYORS OF HIGHEST GOOD
GENERALLY SAY WORDS DESC~
NOTHING BUT IGNORANCE.
LIKE LAO TZE SEZ ~~SAY~~: THEM W
KNOW DON'T SPEAK. A WAG
ADDED LATER /// LAO TZE SEZ ~~~~
WHO ~~KNOW~~ KNOW DON'T SPEAK, BUT IT
TOOK HIM 5000 CHARACTER~
TO SAY IT. HERE IS PARADOX
LANGUAGE. EVEN AS WE SEE IT
IT IS ALWAYS A CASE OF "THIS STATEMENT IS FALSE."
AIN'T GOOD FOR US. WE USE IT WE
SIMULTANEOUSLY OF UPHOLDING THIS PARA
SEE PLAINLY IT POLLUTES MENTA~
WE CAN'T TAKE THE TENSION SO WE
SO FOR FAITH EXPLAIN THIS IS KILLING US SYLOGIS
STILL WE'RE ENAMORED OF IT
OFF AS AN ANIMAL
WE KNOW ABSTRACTIVE
LANGUAGE TO BE THE BASIC CAUS~
OF OUR MISREADING OF NATU~
HOW WE LOST TOUCH, YET THE WAY WE
THINK INVOK ABOUT IT IS: WHAT ELSE IS THE~
PLENTY. PLENTY WHAT? PLENTY MU~
ABSOLUTE.

A SYLLOGISM NO DOUBT

I COULDN'T BRING IT BACK — I WAS AT AN ODD PLACE WHERE THE WAKING STATE SLEEP & THE DREAMSTATE MET & A POEM OR APHORISM OR CALL IT WHAT YOU WILL CAME TO ME — I SET IT OUT IN PERFECT DICTION WITH JUST THE RIGHT WORDS — THE FEELING & IDEA WERE EXPRESSED COMPLETELY IN 3 SHORT SENTENCES — NOW I SAID I'LL WAKE UP AND WRITE IT DOWN — BUT ON THE JOURNEY FROM THERE BACK TO THE WAKING STATE I LOST IT THE POEM OR APHORISM OR CALL IT WHAT YOU WILL — I EVEN WENT BACK TO THE PLACE WHERE IT CAME TO ME & I EVEN FOUND IT AGAIN BUT BRINGING IT BACK I LOST IT AGAIN — YOU WOULD NEVER BELIEVE HOW BEAUTIFUL IT WAS

IS LANGUAGE NECESSARY
TO HUMAN EXISTENCE

LANGUAGE IS A BODY OF SUFFERING & WHEN YOU TAKE UP LANGUAGE YOU TAKE UP THE SUFFERING TOO — US IN WORDS IS INNER VOICE THE CONSTANT COMPANION OF OUR MENTALITY — IT WEIGHS ON OUR CONSCIOUSNESS LIKE A PROBLEM THAT WON'T GO AWAY — NO DOUBT IT'S HANDY THE WAY IT TAKES SOMETHING MOVING AND MAKES IT STILL — AN ARTIFACT THAT CAN BE HELD AND LOOKED AT — THE LANGUAGE DREAM — IT GOES WITH COUNTING — BUT LANGUAGE MAKES US INTO EVERY MEANING IT EXPRESSES SO WE ARE EVERYTHING WE CAN SAY & THIS IS HEAVY — THAT SOMETHING SO OBVIOUSLY ABSTRACT SERIAL & RELATIVE CAN BE SO POWERFUL MAKES YOU WONDER — BUT THE CONSTANT PRESSURE OF WORDS ON PURE MENTALITY ESPECIALLY MEASURED WORDS FINALLY DRIVES EACH OF US MAD IN OUR OWN WAY — IF WE COULD SCREAM

OUT OUR INNER VOICE THEN AS IN TOURETTE'S SYNDROME — WHO HAS NOT BEEN TRAPPED IN A WORD PRISON — WHO DOES NOT KNOW SPIRALING WORD VERTIGO — YET FOR BETTER OR WORSE WE MAKE LANGUAGE # 1 TOOL OF MENTALITY — NO BETTER HERE — MAYBE ALL WORSE — TELL ME A TRUE BENEFIT DERIVING FROM LANGUAGE — CAN A GOOD COME OF IT — PURVEYORS OF HIGHEST GOOD GENERALLY SAY WORDS DESCRIBE NOTHING BUT IGNORANCE — LIKE LAO TZE SEZ THEM WHO KNOW DON'T SPEAK — A WAG ADDED LATER LAO TZE SEZ THEM WHO KNOW DON'T SPEAK BUT IT TOOK HIM 5000 CHARACTERS TO SAY IT — HERE IS PARADOX OF LANGUAGE IT IS ALWAYS A CASE OF THIS STATEMENT IS FALSE — WE CAN'T TAKE THE TENSION OF UPHOLDING THIS PARADOX SO WE GO FOR THE FALSE CERTAINTIES OF SYLLOGISM & THIS IS KILLING US OFF AS AN ANIMAL — EVEN AS WE SEE IT AINT GOOD FOR US WE USE IT — WE SEE PLAINLY IT POLLUTES MENTALITY STILL WE'RE ENAMORED OF IT — WE KNOW

ABSTRACTIVE LANGUAGE TO BE THE BASIC CAUSE OF OUR MISREADING NATURE — HOW WE LOST TOUCH — YET THE WAY WE CONTINUE TO THINK ABOUT IT IS WHAT ELSE IS THERE — PLENTY — PLENTY WHAT — PLENTY MUTE ABSOLUTE

EARTH SLANGUAGE WITH ENGLISH ON IT

I WANT TO WRECK ENGLISH ONCE — ESPECIALLY STOMP ON TEUTONIC ROMANCE JUDEO ROMAN BULLSHIT — LOOSE XTIAN GRIP ON TONGUE — DUMP GREEK AFTER PRESOCRATICS — PULL ENGLISH BACK TOWARD ROOT LANGUAGE OF HOMONID BEFORE CIVILIZATION — I WANT TO CREOLIZE IT — VANDALIZE IT — BEND IT TOWARD CHINESE — A VITAL COMPACT WAY OF SPEAKING & WRITING — SO IT AINT JUST WHITEMAN TALK THAT IS BAD NEWS FOR EVERYONE ELSE — STRIP IT DOWN TO UNIVERSAL GRAMMAR THAT ALL ANIMALS UNDERSTAND — MAKE IT SO THERE'S NO FORMAL-VERNACULAR OR DEMOTIC-HIERATIC OPPOSITION — CUT PUNCTUATION TO DASH — YOU UNDERSTAND WHAT I MEAN — THATS ALL THAT MATTERS — A LINGO ABLE TO EXPRESS MEANING SPARE OR RICHLY TEXTURED — & WHILE WE'RE AT IT LETS MAKE THE WRITTEN LANGUAGE OF THIS COMING UNIVERSAL PIDGIN

MORE PICTOGRAPHIC MORE REBUS-LIKE — MORE HIEROGLYPHIC — SO EVERYONE CAN READ THE FUNNY PAPERS & UNDERSTAND EM — AN EARTH SLANGUAGE UNDERSTOOD BY EVERY HUMAN ON EARTH AS THEIR BIRTHRIGHT TONGUE — SO EVERYONE KNOWS WHAT EVERYONE MEANS & NO MISTAKE — A SLANGUAGE FOR HUMAN POST CIVILIZATION INSTAR

ENGLISH ON IT
I WANT TO WRECK
ENGLISH ONCE — ETRUSCAN ROMAN
STOMP ON TEUTONIC
JUDEO ROMAN BULLSHIT
GREEK AFTER PRE-SOCRATICS I.E. RE-DO INDO-EUROPEAN IN IT
ROMAN
LOOSE ↑ THE XTIAN GRIP ON T
TONGUE * I WANT TO CREOLIZE IT VANDALI
GOOKIFY IT
BEND IT TOWARD CHINE
DEATH
— A VITAL COMPACT WAY
OF SPEAKING or WRITING —
IT AIN'T JUST WHITEMAN TALK THAT IS BAD NEWS
TRIP IT DOWN TO UNIVERSA
FOR EVERYONE ELSE
THAT ALL ANIMALS UNDERSTAND
HAMMER X MAKE IT S
THERE'S NO FORMAL — VERNACU
OR DEMOTIC — HIERATI
OPPOSITION — CUT PUNCTUAT
YOU UNDERSTAND
TO DASH —
THAT I MEAN — THAT'S ALL
THAT MATTERS —
LINGO ABLE TO EXPRESS MEANI
PARE OR RICHLY TEXTURED
WHILE WE'RE AT IT THE WRITTEN
LET'S MAKE COMING UNIVERSAL PIDGIN
OF THIS
LANGUAGE MORE PICTOGRAPH
MORE REBUS-LIKE MORE
SO EVERYONE CAN
A COMMON HIERATIC ONE LANGUA

THE GULF WAR

PUNA — JANUARY 16 1991

EARLY AFTERNOON IN HAWAII
WAR STARTS IN PERSIAN
GULF WITH U.S. AIR-RAID
~~POUNDING SHIT OUTTA~~ ANCIENT BAGHDAD —
RAINS DESTRUCTION ON CRA-
OF CIVILIZATION — MESOPOT-
HIT EM BETWEEN THE OLÉ
TIGRIS & EUPHRATES — N
MERCY FOR THESE LEVANTIN
GOOK ~~MOTHERFUCKERS~~ — EXTERMINA
EM — WE'LL HAVE CANNED
IRAQI MEAT ON THE STOR
SHELVES ~~PRONTO~~ WIKI-WIKI — WHY KILL
ALL THOSE ANIMALS & NO
EAT EM — THERE SO
B~~ACK~~ & L~~A~~IN DOWN THE ROAD THEIR FA-
YELLOW FORD PICK UP TA-
NEAT BUNDLES OF LYCOPOD
TO THEIR NURSERY CONNECT
IN TOWN —

2 BOMBS

1

TERRORIST BOMB

HERE IS A BOMB — IT IS MADE OF WORDS — READ IT & IT GOES OFF IN YOUR HEAD & BLOWS YOU AWAY

2

BOOM

WOKE UP THIS MORNING TO FIND I HAD EXPLODED ALL OVER THE WORLD — I WAS BLOWN TO BITS — I WAS SCATTERED OVER THE WORLD IN SMALL PIECES — WHERE I USED TO BE WAS A BIG EMPTY HOLE THAT FAIRLY REEKED OF PEACE PAST UNDERSTANDING — I COULD NO LONGER SAY I EXISTED YET I WASNT EXACTLY DEAD — I HAD BECOME MYRIAD — EACH SMALL PIECE OF ME HAD REGENERATED INTO ANOTHER WHOLE ME & EACH WHOLE ME WAS STUCK TO

SOME PART OF THE WORLD LIKE GUM OR SNOT
— SO NOW WHEN THE WORLD WIGGLES EVERY
LAST BIT OF ME WIGGLES IN UNISON

THE GULF WAR

1

PUNA — JANUARY 16, 1991

EARLY AFTERNOON IN HAWAI'I WAR STARTS IN PERSIAN GULF WITH U.S. AIR-RAID POUNDING SHIT OUTTA ANCIENT BAGHDAD — BULLY BOY GEORGE GOING TO WHIP SAD SADDAM'S ASS — BULLY BOY GEORGE RAINS DESTRUCTION ON CRADLE OF CIVILIZATION — MESOPOTAMIA — HIT EM BETWEEN THE OLE TIGRIS & EUPHRATES GEORGIE BOY — NO MERCY FOR THESE LEVANTINE GOOK MOTHERFUCKERS — EXTERMINATE EM — WE'LL HAVE CANNED IRAQI MEAT ON STORE SHELVES WIKI WIKI — WHY KILL ALL THOSE ANIMALS & NOT EAT EM — THERE GO B & L DOWN THE ROAD IN THEIR FADED YELLOW FORD PICKUP TAKING NEAT BUNDLES OF LYCOPODIUM TO THEIR NURSERY CONNECTION IN TOWN — THIS CLUB MOSS WITH ITS MINIATURE CONIFER LOOK DOES WELL IN DRY

ARRANGEMENTS — B & L HARVEST THE PLANT OUT OF THE ʻŌHIʻA HĀPUʻU FOREST WE LIVE IN — GOOD PEOPLE HOOKED HEAVY ON BOOZE — THE DAY HAS BEEN SUNNY & CLOUDY BY TURNS WITH SOME LIGHT SHOWERS — A GRAND WINTER DAY IN HAWAIʻI NEI WITH NOBLE PASSAGE OF FAIRWEATHER CUMULUS THROUGH PURE BLUE SKY — SWEET BREATH OF TRADES BLOW LIGHTLY WHILE BACK AT THE RANCH THIS LAST GASP OF WHITE COLONIALISM SOUNDS HORRIFICALLY OVER ARABIA DESERTA — DON'T KNOW ABOUT YOU BUT — ARMAGEDDON OUTTA HERE TO BE NOW WITH CARDINALIS CARDINALIS IN ʻŌHIʻA LEHUA SNAG TOP SINGING WEET WEET WEET WEET — THE CATS & DOG HAVE BEEN QUIET TODAY — FEELING FOR THE CATS & DOGS OF BAGHDAD NO DOUBT — FUCK THE HUMANS — LET EM DO THEIR SLAUGHTER — WE ARE A DESERVEDLY ENDANGERED SPECIES BOUND FOR EXTINCTION — NEIGHBOR HAS MANIAC GENERATOR GOING TO CATCH NEWS ON TUBE

— HIS NEPHEW IN MARINE RESERVES SURE TO BE CALLED UP — I HEAR NEPHEW NEXT DOOR NOW SHOOTING BASKETS WITH HIS COUSIN PATRICK — LAST TIME SAW HIS MOTHER SHE SAID SHE PRAYS & PRAYS WAR NO START — HER PRAYERS NOT ANSWERED — LIGHT RAIN MAKE HOLLOW POCK SOUND ON BANANA LEAVES — BANANAS RIPEN — THE YOUNG UPRIGHT BANANA LEAF WITH RAIN ON IT IS SURELY A WONDROUS BEAUTY OF NATURE — LAURA AT SCHOOL HAS HEARD THE SOLEMN NEWS I'M SURE — SHE'LL BE DISTURBED WHEN I TELL HER THAT HER BROTHER PETER'S SCHOOL IN SINGAPORE RECEIVED A BOMB THREAT YESTERDAY — MUSLIMS THERE TARGET AMERICAN SCHOOL — CHILDREN WERE EVACUATED BUT NO BOMB — LAURA'S MOTHER CALLED FROM IOWA WITH THE NEWS — MEANTIME THE BRANDNEW STANDARD TOYOTA TERCEL 2-DOOR SEDAN WE'RE THINKING OF GETTING WITH ITS LIGHT METALLIC GREEN EXTERIOR & BLACK INTERIOR

IS EVEN NOW MAKING ITS WAY TO HILO PORT FROM JAPAN — DUE IN NEXT WEEK — IF THERE IS A NEXT WEEK — BETTER CANCEL CAR BUY NOW — BUT HEY MOBILITY CONVENIENCE BASED ON CHEAP GAS IS WHAT THIS WAR'S ABOUT YEAH — THE BURSITIS IN MY LEFT SHOULDER HURTS — WHEN LAURA GETS HOME I WILL HOOK INTO AUXILIARY BATTERY MOUNTED ON TRUCK BED & TURN ON RADIO TO HEAR THE GORY DETAILS — GLORY DAYS AHEAD FOR MEDIA — I AM TEMPTED TO GET A TV SET — COLOR OF COURSE — 12 VOLT — THE KIND JUST DRAWS 4 OR 5 AMPS — WANT TO SEE BLOODY SMASHUP IN COLOR — LOTSA BLOODY DETACHED YOUTHFUL LIMBS EYES EARS NOSES & TONGUES SACRIFICED TO DIVINITY — LOTSA MOTHER LIGHT EXPLODING ALL OVER DESERT LIKE NOVAS OF COMPASSION — WELL I GOT THE SWEET POTATOES BOILED FOR SUPPER — I GOT CHOPPED UP CHICKEN CORPSE UNFROZEN — THE GREEN BEANS ARE READY — BRING ON THE WAR

2

WAR & PEACE
A GITA UPDATE IN RHAPSODIC STYLE

IF THE RED SLAYER THINK HE SLAYS,
OR IF THE SLAIN THINK HE IS SLAIN,
THEY KNOW NOT WELL THE SUBTLE WAYS
I KEEP, AND PASS, AND TURN AGAIN.

EMERSON

THE FINAL BODYCOUNT IN GULF WAR — THE FINAL SCORE — U.S. 148 MILITARY DEAD NO CIVILIAN DEAD — IRAQ MILITARY DEAD 100,000 — IRAQ CIVILIAN DEATHS FROM U.S. BOMBS 10,000 — ADD TO THIS THE POST WAR DEATHS ATTRIBUTABLE TO EFFECTS OF WAR SUCH AS INADEQUATE FOOD MEDICINE & MEDICAL CARE TAINTED WATER FROM BUSTED UP WATER & SEWAGE SYSTEMS & DEAD FROM CIVIL STRIFE FOLLOWING WAR ETC — A CONSERVATIVE ESTIMATE WOULD ROUND OUT AT SAY 300,000 + SO THE TOTAL IRAQ BODY COUNT COMES TO

400,000 + — DEVASTATING ESPECIALLY WHEN YOU REMEMBER THAT AFTER THE IRAN-IRAQ WAR 1/2 THE POPULATION OF IRAQ WAS 14 YEARS OLD & UNDER — WOEFUL THE MORTALITY RATE OF CHILDREN 5 YEARS OLD & YOUNGER — WE TRASHED IRAQI YOUTH — US & THE IRANIANS — AND THE DYING AINT OVER YET — THEIR MANHOOD AINT GOING TO RECOVER FOR A LONG TIME — THIS IS HYPER CYBERNETICAL WAR — 86,000 TONS OF BOMBS DROPPED IN 43 DAYS — A NEW WORLD RECORD — THAT'S ONE BOMB OR MISSILE EVERY 15 SECONDS ON AVERAGE — ABOUT 250,000 BOMBS & MISSILES DELIVERED BY AIR — INCLUDING SUCH GEMS OF THE ART OF WEAPONRY AS THE CLUSTER BOMB THAT SPEWED OUT RAZOR SHARP BOMBLETS THAT CAN PUNCH THRU ARMORED VEHICLES KILLING & MAIMING THOSE WITHIN — THE FUEL AIR EXPLOSIVES THAT WORK BY SPRAYING AN EXPLOSIVE MIST OVER TARGET & IGNITING IT GENERATING BLAST WAVE THAT CAN EXCEED 400 LBS PER SQ INCH

ENUFF TO CRUSH BUNKERS & FLIP OVER 60 TON TANKS — YOU BETTER BELIEVE IT'S THE FASTEST WAY TO CLEAR A MINEFIELD — 5 LBS PER SQ INCH WILL EXPLODE HUMAN LUNGS — THIS SUCKER IS SO BIG IT HAS TO BE PUSHED OUT THE END OF A C-130 CARGO PLANE — OR HOW ABOUT THE 4700 LB BOMB FILLED WITH EXPLOSIVE GOODIES THAT HAS HARDENED STEEL CAP THAT CAN BURROW 100 FT BELOW SURFACE OF GROUND BEFORE EXPLODING — PERFECT FOR BURIED COMMAND BUNKERS — SO — DID WE WHIP THEIR ASS OR NOT — 148 TO 400,000 + & STILL COUNTING — SOME SCORE — ANOTHER WORLD RECORD FOR DESTRUCTION BY U.S. AIR POWER — ACCORDING TO GREENPEACE IRAQI DEATHS AVERAGED MORE THAN ONE PERSON PER EVERY TON OF EXPLOSIVES WHICH IS TWICE AS EFFICIENT A RATE OF KILLING AS THE AVERAGE OF ONE PERSON PER EVERY 2 TONS OF EXPLOSIVES IN VIETNAM — IT WAS A MOTHER OF A WAR & NO MISTAKE — WE BLASTED EM PRACTICALLY BACK TO THE FUCKIN STONE AGE

— WE ALSO WIPED OUT A LOT OF ARCHEOLOGY — SO WHAT — LIKE HENRY FORD SEZ HISTORY IS BUNK — & WHAT'S ARCHEOLOGY BUT THE HISTORY OF OTHER GULF WARS BACK THRU THE EARLIEST PAGES OF POOR BEDRAGGLED RECORDED TIME & BEFORE LIKE FOSSILS TELL US — WORSE IS WHAT WE DID TO THE ENVIRONMENT — NATURE GETS NO RESPECT FROM HOMO SAPIENS WHEN IT COMES TO ALL OUT WAR — ARMIES DON'T HAVE TO WRITE ENVIRONMENTAL IMPACT STATEMENTS BEFORE THEIR WARS — IF THEY DID THERE WOULD NOT BE WARS — NATURE COMES BACK BUT WE TORE UP IRAQ SOMETHING SPECIAL US & SADDAM — HERE LET US GIVE A SHORT WAIL FOR THE GONE BIOME OF MESOPOTAMIA & FOR THE GONE WATERS OF PERSIAN GULF — HUMANS HAVE BEEN AROUND MESOPOTAMIA FOR A LONG TIME & THEY HAD THE PLACE WORN DOWN TO A NUB LONG BEFORE GEORGE PUSHED THE BUTTON ON EM BUT WE SURE MESSED UP WHAT WAS LEFT OF THE PLACE — THINK OF THE BIRDS BLASTED OUT

OF THEIR FEATHERS — THE INSECTS WHOPPED
OUT OF THEIR SKELETONS BY THE JILLIONS —
ALL OF THE CREATURES THAT INHABIT THE
GROUND SQUASHED BY BOMB HITTING GROUND
— THE FUCKING MAMMALS FROM MICE TO
HUMANS WHAPPED OUT OF THEIR SKULLS BY
THE TENS & HUNDREDS OF THOUSANDS EVEN
MILLIONS I VENTURE TO SAY — THE SHRUBS
BLASTED OFF THEIR ROOTS — THE BLASTED
SPLINTERED TREES — FORGET WHAT WE DID TO
THE FLOWERING PLANTS — ONE MINUTE THEIR
FACE TO THE SUN THE NEXT MINUTE BLASTED
TO NOTHING EVEN THEIR FRAGRANCE — THINK
OF THE STARTLED SKY — AND THE WAY WE DID
IT — PUSH BUTTON WAR — WE COULD HAVE
FOUGHT IT WITH WHITE GLOVES ON — O WHAT
YOU CAN DO WHEN YOUR ENEMY HAS NO AIR
FORCE OR NAVY NO STATE OF THE ART
ROCKETRY TO SPEAK OF & IS A LOT SMALLER
THAN YOU WITH A POPULATION 50% UNDER THE
AGE OF 14 — WE GAVE EM ALL THE STUFF WE
WERE SAVING FOR THE RUSSIANS — GOT RID OF

A LOT OF OLD INVENTORY IN BOMBS & SUCH & GAVE BOMB MAKERS A REAL SHOT IN THE ARM — WHAT A WONDERFUL COMMODITY — YOU CAN ONLY USE IT ONCE — THAT'S ALL THE LONGER IT LASTS — IT'S A THROWAWAY ITEM — IF YOU LIKE WHAT IT DID & YOU WANT TO DO IT AGAIN YOU HAVE TO BUY A NEW ONE — & IT'S A COMMODITY LIKE SALT — EVERYBODY WANTS & NEEDS IT — A TRILLION $ INDUSTRY WORLDWIDE — MERCHANTS OF DEATH MOST NECESSARY TO CIVILIZATION — HAVE YOU EVER HEARD OF A CIVILIZATION THAT DID NOT WAGE WAR — LIKE ALWAYS IT'S A MERCHANTS OF DEATH SCIENCE GOVT COMBO — NOW SCIENCE HAS BECOME THE MAJOR PLAYER — THEY GOT SOME FINE PEOPLE WORKING ON THESE MARVELOUS INVENTIONS FOR EXTERMINATION OF CONSPECIFICS IN MASSIVE NUMBERS — 99% OF ALL THE SCIENTISTS WHO HAVE EVER LIVED LIVE NOW & 1/3 OF EM ARE WORKING ON WAR BETTERMENT PROJECTS — KEEP EM COMING BOYS — WE CAN ALWAYS USE MORE & BETTER

BOMBS — I LIKE YOUR IDEA OF THE NEUTRON BOMB THAT ONLY KILLS LIFE & LEAVES REAL ESTATE INTACT — THAT WAY WE CAN USE THE CONQUERED PLACE FOR AT LEAST A PENAL COLONY THUS RELIEVING OUR EVER MORE CROWDED PRISONS — & THE PRISONERS CAN CLEAN UP THE BOMB AFTERMATH — THAT IS — IF NONE OF THE REST OF US WANT TO MOVE & SETTLE THERE FOR CALL EM ESTHETIC REASONS — LIKE WHAT ABOUT ALL THOSE CORPSES OF THE FORMER ENEMY — THIS IS THE WEAKNESS OF THE NEUTRON BOMB — ALL THE FORMER INHABITANTS ARE DEAD — CAUGHT IN THE POSTURE OF THEIR LAST ACT — GORE AMONGST INTACT INFRASTRUCTURE REAL ESTATE & PERSONAL PROPERTY — & THE ROADS ARE CLOGGED WITH CORPSES — OCCUPYING TROOPS CAN'T MOVE — TREAT EM LIKE ROADKILLS — THEY'RE DEAD — JUST DRIVE AROUND OR OVER EM AS YOU WOULD WITH ANY ROADKILL — FIRST THE CORPSE GETS SQUASHED FLAT — MESSY AT FIRST BUT THEN IT DRIES OUT — GETS

SHREDDED — THEN IT DISAPPEARS — YOU'VE SEEN IT HAPPEN — VANISHES INTO THIN AIR — OR HERE'S ANOTHER IDEA LETS BE FRANK IS THERE A SHORTAGE OF ORGANS FOR ORGAN TRANSPLANTS OR NOT — FIRST THING AFTER BOMB DROP IN GO OUR ORGAN EXTRACTOR MEDICO COMMANDOS & DEEP FREEZE UNITS — NEED I SAY MORE — A TRUE YANKEE WILL MAKE EVEN THE AFTERMATH OF WAR PAY IF HE CAN — GROSS MAN GROSS — BUT MY FRIEND WAR IS GROSS — THINK OF WHAT A SIMPLE A-BOMB DOES TO PEOPLE — KABOOM — AT GROUND ZERO FIRST THERE'S THERMAL RADIATION FROM FIREBALL OF SUPERHEATED AIR AROUND DETONATION — 2 PULSES ARE EMITTED — HEAT FROM 1ST PULSE DESTROYS THE EYES — THE SECOND PULSE MELTS FLESH — THE HIROSHIMA SURVIVOR DR HACHIYA SAW PEOPLE WITH THE FEATURES OF THEIR FACES MELTED TOGETHER — THEN A SHOCK WAVE OF HIGH PRESSURE & EXPANDING GASES CAUSES UNBELIEVABLE WINDS THAT LITERALLY RIP FLESH FROM BODY

— SHOCK WAVE OVERPRESSURE THEN SQUASHES BODY CAUSING ORGANS TO HEMORRHAGE & RUPTURE — TO FINISH OFF THERE'S RADIATION BY INHALATION INGESTION & ABSORPTION — GHASTLY — SCIENTIFIC HYPERWAR — YOU GOT CIVILIZATION YOU GOT WAR — IT'S A GIVEN OF THE CIVILIZED STATE — BUT NOW WOULDN'T IT BE AN ADVANCE FOR CIVILIZATION IF WE COULD TAKE THE GORE OUT OF WAR — WHAT WE NEED GUYS IS A SUPER SMART BOMB THAT WILL DISCRIMINATE THE HUMAN OUT OF THE REST OF NATURE & DESTROY ONLY THE HUMAN — DESTROY BY VAPORIZATION — BOMB WILL TAKE BODY OF ENEMY FROM SOLID TO GASEOUS STATE IN AN INSTANT WHILE OF COURSE LIKE THE NEUTRON BOMB IT WILL LEAVE THE INFRASTRUCTURE REAL ESTATE PERSONAL PROPERTY ETC INTACT — WHEN BOMB GOES OFF IT TURNS JUST HUMANS INTO INNOCUOUS PUFFS OF STEAM THAT DISAPPEAR INTO THE ATMOSPHERE WITHOUT LEAVING A TRACE NOT EVEN A BAD

ODOR — THE VERY ATMOSPHERE WE BREATHE — NO THIS IS NOT CANNIBALISM BY INHALATION — IT IS COMPLETELY SANITARY WAR — THINK OF IT ONE BOMB & ALL THE ENEMY ARE DEAD & THERE ARE NO CORPSES — AFTER THE BOMB WE WON'T NEED SOLDIERS TO INVADE & OCCUPY OUR NEW TERRITORY — WE WILL SIMPLY SEND IN OUR TOURIST-COLONISTS — THESE INSOUCIANT CONQUERORS WILL SAUNTER INTO OUR NEWLY ACQUIRED LAND & TAKE OVER THE INTACT EMPTY CITIES TOWNS VILLAGES & SUBURBS OF OUR FORMER ENEMY — IT WILL BE LIKE THE FORMER INHABITANTS OF THIS LAND HAD JUST STEPPED OUT — BUT THEY WON'T BE COMING BACK — YOU MAY BE SURE OF THAT — THERE WILL BE CASH IN THE BANKS & FOOD IN EVERY FRIDGE & ON STORE SHELVES — CARS & PUBLIC TRANSIT READY TO GO — INFRASTRUCTURE INTACT — PLENTY OF EMPTY HOUSES CONDOS & APARTMENTS — DON'T TAKE A SUITCASE — EVERYTHING YOU NEED IS THERE — JUST FIND YOUR SIZE — THE SUN OF OUR SKY

IS BRIGHT & WARM THERE — BIRDS SING IN THE TREES WHOSE LEAVES SHED THE CLEAR BRILLIANT LIGHT & CAST WELCOME SHADE TO GROUND — THE BOMB SOMEHOW CAUSES SPRINGS OF CLEAR PURE RUNNING WATER TO BURST OUT OF GROUND ALL OVER THE LANDSCAPE — THESE LOW FOUNTS OF WATER ARE LIKE EYES OF COMPASSION — THE BOMB WILL ALSO CLEANSE ALL REAL ESTATE & PERSONAL PROPERTY SO OUR FASTIDIOUS CONQUEROR MAN WOMAN OR CHILD CAN CLAIM & HANDLE BOOTY WITHOUT FEAR OF NOXIOUS INFECTIONS — NOW THIS IS WAR — ONE BOMB THEN PEACE IMMEDIATELY — AND THE CONQUERED LAND JUST SITTING THERE INTACT EMPTY SANITARY & PRETTY READY FOR OUR STALWARTS — ONE BIG PERFECTLY PRESERVED ARTIFACT OF FORMER ENEMY'S DOMAIN WITH FORMER ENEMY ARTIFICERS GONE — AND SO FORTH — NUFF SAID ABOUT BOMBS — LET ME TELL YOU THIS WAR HAS TAUGHT ME ONE THING — AS LONG AS THERE

ARE HUMANS ORGANIZED INTO NATION-STATES THERE'S GOING TO BE WARS ON EARTH — I THINK I FINALLY GOT THE LESSON — LIKE TOLSTOY SAID WAR & PEACE — A COMBO — YOU DONT GET ONE WITHOUT THE OTHER — TOGETHER THEY COMPRISE CIVILIZATION — INDEED THESE TWIN CONSTANTS OF NATION-STATES ARE THE VERY STUFF OF CIVILIZATION — & LET ME STATE HERE AS A CIVILIZED HUMAN THAT I WILL BE WANTING BOTH MY WARS & MY PEACE — PEACE IS FOR RECOVERING FROM WARS — WARS ARE FOR YEARNING FOR PEACE — THEY BALANCE OUT TO WHAT WE CALL NORMAL CIVILIZED BEHAVIOR — THE STORY OF THE ANATOMICALLY MODERN HUMAN WHO HAS BEEN AROUND 100,000 YRS IS A STORY OF WAR & PEACE — EVEN BEFORE CIVILIZATION HOMO WAS ON OVERKILL TRIP — THIS HAS BEEN GOING ON FOR THE 100,000 YRS WE BEEN AROUND — THE 1ST GREAT WAR EXPERIENCE OF HOMO WAS WHEN WE BROKE THE STRONGEST TABOO IN THE ANIMAL WORLD — THE ONE THAT FORBADE

KILLING BEYOND NEED — THIS IS WHEN WE 1ST DECLARED WAR ON THE BIOME & TOOK UP TEAM THRILL OVERKILL DOMINATION OF REST OF NATURE TRIP WE ARE STILL ON — SUBSISTENCE KILL IS NORM — IT IS PART OF THE DESIGN & ECONOMY OF NATURE — KILLING BEYOND NEED AS IN TEAM THRILL OVERKILL IS MALADAPTIVE CUZ IT'S ULTIMATELY SELF DESTRUCTIVE — HOMO BROKE OUT OF PEACEABLE KINGDOM IN WHICH ANIMALS EAT ANIMALS IN DEEP PEACE & PROCEEDED TO SLAUGHTER THE MEGAFAUNA THOSE ANIMALS 100 LB + ADULT WEIGHT & EXTERMINATED THE GIANT FAUNA ASSEMBLAGE OF MAMMOTH WOOLY RHINOCEROUS GIANT DEER HORSE BISON ET AL OVER ALL OF EURASIAN & N & S AMERICAN CONTINENTS — SAME STORY OVER REST OF WORLD BUT TO LESSER DEGREE — THE QUATERNARY EXTINCTIONS THE COMPARATIVELY SUDDEN DISAPPEARANCE OF A LARGE PERCENTAGE OF MEGA & GIANT FAUNA OVER MOST OF THE WORLD DURING THE LATE PLEISTOCENE — THAT

IS DURING THE LAST 100,000 YRS — COINCIDENT WITH APPEARANCE OF MODERN HS ON SCENE — AT FIRST THE EXTINCTIONS ARE SLOW THEN THEY BEGIN A GRADUAL INCREASE TO ABOUT 35,000 YRS BP WHEN EXTINCTION RATE SPEEDS UP TO CLIMAX 11,000 YRS BP IN THE MASSIVE OVERKILL OF THE N & S AMERICAN MEGA & GIANT FAUNA — THESE EXTINCTIONS FOLLOW THE TRACK OF MODERN HOMO THROUGH THE MIDDLE EAST INTO ASIA & EUROPE ACROSS THE EURASIAN PLAIN SIBERIA & ACROSS BERINGIAN LAND BRIDGE TO N & S AMERICA — TEAM THRILL OVERKILL ALL THE WAY — BUT SO FAR WE'VE COVERED ONLY HOMO SAP VS OTHER ANIMALS — BLOODY ENUFF OF AN ENCOUNTER FOR SURE — NOTHING LESS THAN ONE KIND OF ANIMAL THRASHING OTHER ANIMALS IN A KIND OF WAR — TEAM THRILL OVERKILL — A TOTALLY INAPPROPRIATE RESPONSE TO THE SURROUND — THE VERY DEFINITION OF PSYCHOTIC — NOW ON TOP OF THIS WAR HOMO SAPIENS WAS WAGING YET ANOTHER WAR — THIS ONE AGAINST THE

OTHER HOMONID SPECIES OF THE TIME IN EURASIA — NEANDERTHAL — CRO-MAGNON — ARCHAIC MAN A RACE TRANSITIONAL TO HUMAN OUT OF HOMO ERECTUS — ARCHAIC HUMAN IS IN FOSSIL RECORD FROM 300,000 TO 35,000 YRS BP — THE TYPE OF THIS HUMAN IS SWANSCOMBE HUMAN — NEANDERTHAL HUMAN FIRST APPEARS IN FOSSIL RECORD 125,000 YRS BP & DISAPPEARS ABRUPTLY 35,000 YRS BP — CRO-MAGNON IS IN THE FOSSIL RECORD FROM 35,000 YRS BP TO 10,000 YRS BP WHEN THEY TOO DISAPPEAR SUDDENLY — SO ONCE THERE WERE 4 HOMONID SPECIES ON THE EURASIAN CONTINENT AT THE SAME TIME — WHAT AN INTERESTING TABLEAU THIS SUGGESTS — TRULY LET 100 HOMONID TYPES THRIVE & FLOWER TOGETHER — OR SO YOU WOULD THINK — I CAN'T THINK OF A CLIMATE-ECOCHANGE MODEL THAT WOULD DISALLOW ALL 4 HOMONID SPECIES FROM COEXISTING & SURVIVING TO THE PRESENT DAY — I CAN THINK OF A CULTURAL MODEL FOR IT NOT HAPPENING

— INTRAMURAL HOMONID WARS — THESE ARE THE FIRST HUMAN WARS — IF WE INTERJECT HERE THE FACT THAT MOST LARGE MAMMAL CARCASSES FOUND IN EURASIA & ALASKA DATE TO TWO PERIODS 45,000–30,000 YRS BP & 14,000–10,000 YRS BP ALL THE NUMBERS FALL INTO PLACE & AN INTERESTING STORYLINE SUGGESTS ITSELF — HOMO SAP ARRIVES IN EURASIA 100,000 YRS BP & COMMENCES TO BREAK ANIMAL TABOO AGAINST OVERKILL — OTHER HOMONIDS SEE MEGAFAUNA & ESPECIALLY GIANT FAUNA BEGINNING TO DISAPPEAR BEFORE THEIR EYES — THEY CATCH OVERKILL FEVER — ALL HOMONIDS BREAK OVERKILL TABOO — A DEADLY COMPETITION ENSUES AMONG THEM — FREEFORALL OVERKILL EXTERMINATIONS FOLLOW IN WHICH ARCHAIC HOMO & NEANDERTHAL DISAPPEAR ABRUPTLY — THIS HAPPENS 45–35,000 YRS BP — HOMO SAP & CRO-MAG HOMO SURVIVE — IT IS NOW ESTABLISHED AS OK TO SLAUGHTER FELLOW HOMONIDS IN PURSUIT OF LEBENSRAUM — A

GIANT STEP TOWARD CIVILIZATION — HOMO SAP & CRO-MAG MAN COEXIST FOR 25,000 YRS — THE OVERKILL ON LARGE MAMMALS CONTINUES TILL AROUND 15–10,000 YRS BP BY WHICH TIME A LARGE PART OF THE NORTHERN EURASIAN MEGAFAUNA & ALMOST ALL THE GIANT FAUNA HAS BEEN WIPED OUT — ANOTHER DEADLY COMPETITION ENSUES FOR THE LAST OF THIS ONCE MAGNIFICENT ANIMAL ASSEMBLAGE — THIS TIME IT'S THE BIG ONE — IT'S FOR THE WORLD HOMONID CHAMPIONSHIP — HOMO SAP VS CRO-MAG MAN — TURNS OUT NO CONTEST — WE SMOTHER EM WITH OUR NUMBERS — THEY — HOW SHALL WE PUT IT — THEY GO EXTINCT ABRUPTLY — CRO-MAGNON WAS SMARTER THAN US — HAD A BIGGER BRAIN — CRO-MAGNON KNEW ANIMALS OUR SIZE MAKE SENSE ONLY AT SMALLER POPULATIONS — THEY KEPT THEIR POP DOWN — THEY WERE TOO SMART FOR THEIR OWN GOOD — THEY SHOULD HAVE KNOWN US HOMO SAPIENS DON'T BELIEVE ANY KIND OF ENVIRONMENTALIST BULLSHIT —

NEVER HAVE NEVER WILL — SO BY 10,000 YRS BP HOMO SAP IS ICHIBAN ANIMAL & SOLE HOMONID ON EARTH — WE ARE STILL ON TOP — THERE ARE OVER 5 1/2 BILLIONS OF US ON EARTH TODAY & OUR POPULATION STILL GROWS THO EVERY SIGN SEZ SUBZEROPOP NOW — 5 1/2 BILLION MEGASIZE ANIMALS OF ONE SPECIES & EVERY SINGLE ONE OF US ON AN OVERKILL DOMINATION TRIP OF SOME KIND AT SOME LEVEL WITH REGARD TO OUR SURROUNDING BIOME & THE REST OF EARTH NATURE — OVERKILL TABOO BROKEN ACROSS THE BOARD — OPEN SEASON ON SLAUGHTER OF EVERY LIFE FORM THAT GETS IN OUR WAY INCLUDING CONSPECIFICS — IT'S AWESOME — WE THINK IT'S OK — WE KEEP DOING IT — BUT BEFORE WE GET INTO A GUILTY FUNK ABOUT IT LETS REMEMBER HOMO SAPIENS IS NOT THE ONE WHO STARTED THIS VIOLENCE & MAYHEM ON EARTH — HOMO SAP DID NOT INVENT THE WEAPON — HOMO HABILIS INVENTED THE WEAPON & EVERY HOMO TYPE SINCE HAS IMPROVED THE WEAPON — H

HABILIS TAKES US BACK 2 MILL YRS — SO HEY OUR OMNICIDAL TRIP AINT EVEN OUR FAULT — IT'S THOSE OTHER FUCKING GIANT APES THAT STARTED IT — H HABILIS HOMO ERECTUS ET AL — IF THEY HAD BEEN MORE PEACEFUL WE WOULDN'T BE THE WAY WE ARE — THAT'S HOMONID KARMA — SO SINCE THRU NO FAULT OF OUR OWN WE'RE ON THIS BLOODY PATH BEQUEATHED TO US BY SAID ANCESTORS LETS DO IT RIGHT — I SAY SCIWAR — PURE HITECH HYPERWAR — I'M FOR STARWARS — PUSH BUTTON WAR — SANITARY — WHITE GLOVES — RED TELEPHONE — BRIEFCASE WITH CODED COUNTDOWN — PRERECORDED MESSAGE IN CRYPTEXT DECLARING WAR — HUMAN VAPORIZER BOMB DIRECT TO YOU FROM OUTER SPACE MOTHERFUCKERS — PRESS BUTTON — BOMBS AWAY — WITHIN A FEW MINUTES OR LESS THE WAR IS OVER — NEAT — KLEEN — NO LONGER DO WE NEED ARMY NAVY AIR FORCE MARINE CORPS — MOTHBALL EM — WARRIOR BULLSHIT OLD FASHIONED — LEAVE IT TO THE SCIENTISTS

— GIVE US THE V-BOMB HUH GUYS RIGHT AWAY BEFORE SOMEONE ELSE INVENTS IT — & LETS BE LIBERAL IN OUR APPLICATION OF SCIWAR — ONE TIME 100,000 TO 200,000 DEAD AT A MINIMUM — BUT NOW HOW DO WE DEAL WITH THE QUALM WE FEEL WHEN WE THINK OF VICTIM POPULATION — ALL THOSE PEOPLE WHO'VE BEEN VAPORIZED FOR OUR SAKE — RETHINK DEATH — RETHINK DEATH — LETS RETHINK DEATH — MAYBE DEATH HAS HAD UNDESERVED BAD PRESS — CONSTANT BAD RAP ABOUT WHAT A DOWNER IT IS COMPARED TO LIVING & HOW IT'S TO BE AVOIDED AT ALL COST — DO WE OVERRATE LIFE — IT MAY BE AMA PROPAGANDA — DR SEZ WE'LL WARD DEATH OFF YA AWFUL AWFUL DEATH FOR AS LONG AS WE CAN CUZ YOU DON'T WANNA DIE DO YOU IN FACT EVEN IF YOU'RE BRAIN DEAD WE'LL KEEP THAT TICKER GOING DONT WORRY ABOUT IT CUZ IT'S OUR FIRM BELIEF BETTER BRAINDEAD THAN DEAD — BUT IS DEATH AWFUL — LETS FACE IT WE ARE BORN TO DIE — THERE'S BIRTH THEN SOME

JUNKY STUFF LIKE SUFFERING & SOME DEEP TRULY DEEP PLAISANCE THEN WACKO DEATH — WE GOTTA DIE NO MATTER WHICH WAY WE LOOK AT IT — WHAT IF DEATH AINT AWFUL — WHAT IF DEATH IS AN UTTERLY BEAUTIFUL EUPHORIC TRANSFORMING BEATIFIC PAINLESS EVENT IN WHICH ALL THINGS ARE EXPLAINED & THERE IS PEACE PAST UNDERSTANDING LIKE RELIGIONISTS HAVE BRAGGED FOR MILLENIA — WHAT IF LIFE IS OVERRATED & DEATH UNDERRATED — WE HAVE A STRONG BODY OF EVIDENCE HERE INDICATING THE DEATH EXPERIENCE MAY NOT BE AWFUL — WE ARE NOT TALKING ABOUT DYING — DYING IS A FORM OF LIVING — DEATH IS AN EVENT UNTO ITSELF — ANYONE WHO HAS DIED IN THE WAKING STATE IN BROAD DAYLIGHT OR IN LUCID DREAM OR ANYONE WHO HAS HAD AN OUT OF BODY EXPERIENCE OF ANY KIND CAN TELL YOU THAT THE MOMENT OF RELEASE FROM BODY SPARKS THE THOT IS THIS WHAT ALL PEOPLE FEAR AS ONE MOVES FROM BODY TO EASEFUL EUPHORIC

COMPASSIONATE ZERO MASS COGNITIVE MODE OF DEATH EVENT — ANYONE WHO HAS KEPT VIGIL BESIDE A STRONG PERSON DYING A NATURAL UNDRUGGED DEATH AT HOME CAN SEE IT IS A TOTALLY TRANSFORMING EXPERIENCE AWESOME IN ITS BEAUTY & SIMPLICITY — THE GRAND LEAP PAST THE LAST BREATH — WHEN BLAKE'S BROTHER ROBERT DIED BLAKE SAW HIS SPIRIT RISE THROUGH THE CEILING CLAPPING HIS ZERO MASS HANDS FOR JOY — IT WOULD BE LIKE SHIFTING INTO OVERDRIVE ON A FLAT STRAIGHT ROAD — MY NEIGHBOR A MAN IN HIS 80'S FROM THE PHILIPPINES SEZ HE'S NOT AFRAID TO DIE BECUZ HE ALREADY DIED & IT WAS BEAUTIFUL — AS A CHILD HE FELL SICK WITH HIGH FEVER & HE DIED — HE LEFT HIS BODY & ENTERED A TUNNEL WITH LIGHT AT THE END — WHEN HE CAME INTO THE LIGHT HE WAS IN PARADISE — HE WAS IN A MEADOW SURROUNDED BY WOODED HILLS — OUT OF THE HILLS RAN A STREAM FULL SWIFT & CLEAR — ON ONE BANK OF THE STREAM WERE

GATHERED ALL HIS ANCESTORS & THEY GREETED & EMBRACED HIM — THEN AFTER THEY HAD TALKED STORY FOR AWHILE THEY TOLD HIM THAT HE MUST RETURN TO THE LIVING — HE DID NOT WANT TO LEAVE — THEY SAID IT WAS NOT HIS TIME — SO HE CAME BACK — DEATH HERE IS IMMEDIATE BIRTH TO NEXT MODE — NO MATTER THE DEATH CAUSE BE VIOLENT OR SUBDUED DEATH ITSELF HAPPENS TO EVERY ORGANISM IN THE SAME WAY — WHETHER GETTING VAPORIZED BY THE V-BOMB OR DYING IN BOSOM OF FAMILY WITH BENEFIT OF CLERGY IT IS THE SAME EVENT — THE SHIFT FROM EMBODIED COG MODE TO BODILESS COG MODE IS ALWAYS A BLISS-RAPTURE EVENT — & THIS GETTING FROM HARD DIMENSIONAL MODE INTO INVISIBLE BLISS MODE IS ALWAYS FELT AS A TRANSITION FROM ONE SPACE TO A FAR BETTER SPACE PARTICULARLY IN THE SPHERES OF UNDERSTANDING & COMPASSION & THEN THERE IS ITS INCOMPARABLE LIGHTNESS — THAT DEATH SHOULD BE FULL OF VIRTUE BEAUTY &

UNDERSTANDING SEEMS ALTOGETHER NATURAL — WERE THIS NOT SO DEATH WOULD NOT HAVE SURVIVED EVOLUTIONARILY AMONG ANIMALS AS NO ANIMAL WOULD LONG CONSENT TO DIE WERE NOT DEATH EQUAL TO OR BETTER THAN LIFE — IN SHORT DEATH HAS EVER BEEN & EVER WILL BE GOOD NEWS HOWEVER IT IS DELIVERED — DEATH IS GOOD NEWS — THE BEST NEWS — SO WHEN YOU DROP THE V-BOMB ON EM THINK OF IT AS 100,000 TO 200,000 PEOPLE GETTING THE BEST NEWS THEY EVER GOT IN THEIR WHOLE LIVES — LETS GET ON WITH IT — BOMBS AWAY

TO IRISH HEROES

YOU SAID WE WILL NOT ALLOW OUR BODIES & PERSONS TO BE USED BY THOSE WHO OPPRESS US TO THE EXTENT OF STRIPPING US TO THE CONDITION OF ANIMALS IN A ZOO CAGE — WE ARE GOING TO SHOW FOREIGN OPPRESSOR STATE THAT INDIVIDUALS STILL REIGN SUPREME — YOU STOPPED EATING — YOU FASTED TO THE DEATH ONE AFTER THE OTHER — YOU MADE THE SUPREME STATEMENT OF POLITICAL DISSENT — NO STATE OWNS ME — I KNOW HOW IT WENT — AT FIRST IT WAS RESOLVE OF HATRED FOR OPPRESSOR — AS FAST WENT ON YOU WERE SURPRISED — YOU SAW HUMAN LIFE WAS A VAIL OF TEARS & YOU WEPT — THEN TOWARD THE END EYE OF COMPASSION SUDDENLY POPPED OPEN & OPPRESSOR STATE BECAME INDIVIDUALS LIKE YOURSELVES ANGELIC & INNOCENT LIKE YOURSELVES & HAD YOU THE STRENGTH THEN YOU WOULD HAVE RUN TO EACH ONE & EMBRACED THEM SAYING BROTHER FORGIVE ME

FOR BEING A MAN — I KNOW THE POWERS OF THE LONG FAST — HAD I YOUR CAUSE THEN I WOULD HAVE GLADLY JOINED YOU TO THE LAST BREATH

PROCRUSTES
A RANT

1

ACCORDING TO MY WEBSTER'S INTERNATIONAL DICTIONARY THE WORD PROCRUSTEAN COMES FROM THE PRACTICE OF AN ANCIENT GREEK ROBBER PROCRUSTES WHO FORCED HIS VICTIMS TO FIT A CERTAIN BED BY STRETCHING OR CUTTING OFF THEIR LEGS — THE FAMOUS PROCRUSTES' BED — WEBSTER'S DEFINITION OF THE WORD GOES AS FOLLOWS — PROCRUSTEAN THAT IS MARKED BY COMPLETE DISREGARD OF INDIVIDUAL DIFFERENCES OR SPECIAL CIRCUMSTANCES AND THAT ARBITRARILY OFTEN RUTHLESSLY OR VIOLENTLY FORCES INTO CONFORMITY WITH OR SUBSERVIENCE TO SOMETHING AS A SYSTEM POLICY DOCTRINE — ISN'T PROCRUSTEAN THE VERY DEFINITION OF GOVT — WITH GOVT WE ALL GOT OUR LEGS CHOPPED OFF OR STRETCHED TO SIZE AVERAGE & WE ARE ALL HOBBLING ALONG LIKE WE DON'T

MIND IT — I HAVE COME TO MIND BEING GOVERNED — I HAVE COME TO MIND LIVING UNDER A REGIMEN I HAD NO SAY IN JOINING OR NOT JOINING — NO SOONER WAS I BORN THAN I'M AUTOMATICALLY RECRUITED INTO CITIZENSHIP & ALL THE GOD AWFUL DUTIES THAT GO WITH IT — I HAVE COME TO MIND THE WEIGHT OF GOVT ON MY ANIMAL NATURE — I'M ASTONISHED AT THE POWERS THE U.S. CONSTITUTION GIVES WHAT ARE CALLED THE EXECUTIVE LEGISLATIVE & JUDICIAL BRANCHES OF GOVT OVER ME & MY PRIVATE ANIMAL FATE — IT SEZ PLAINLY THEY CONSIDER ME TO BE A SLAVE OF THEIR STATE — I DON'T NEED THESE PEOPLE & THEIR FUCKING GAMES IN MY LIFE — WHO ARE THESE PEOPLE WHO ACTUALLY BELIEVE THEY KNOW BETTER THAN ME WHATS GOOD FOR ME & WHO WILL TAKE THIS WHATS GOOD FOR ME THAT THEY KNOW BETTER THAN ME & MAKE LAWS ABOUT IT THAT THEY BACK UP WITH GUNS & CAGES BELIEVE IT OR NOT — THEY GOT NO HUMOR — THEY GOT NO RESPECT FOR

ANYTHING BUT RULING BY THEIR FUCKING LAWS — THEY'RE ASSHOLES BECUZ NOBODY BUT ASSHOLES WOULD SET THEMSELVES UP AS ARBITERS OF SOMEONE ELSE'S BEHAVIOR — I DECLARE MYSELF TO BE FREE OF THEM — I DECLARE MYSELF TO BE A FREE ANIMAL ON EARTH — LET ME TELL YOU WHO I AM

2

I AM A REED THAT CEPHALIZED & GREW LIMBS — I AM THE ANIMAL THAT I AM & NOT A BIRD OR FISH — I AM UP ON MY HIND LEGS — I AM SCANNING MY SURROUND WITH TRICHROMATIC BINOCULAR VISION THAT GIVES ME 4D IN COLOR — EARTH THRIVES BEFORE ME WITH STUPENDOUS ECLAT SO IT ACTUALLY SEEMS REAL IT SHINES SO WITH BEING — MY EYES ARE SET TO FRONT IN VERTICAL FACE WITH DOMED FOREHEAD — I SHARE BREATH WITH EARTH — I AM BREATHING COMMON AIR LADEN WITH VARIOUS FRAGRANCE OF SURROUND — DID I NOT BREATHE AIR I WOULD BE ANAEROBIC OR

ANGELIC — MY TONGUE LIES IN DARK CAVERN OF MOUTH WAITING TO CALL OUT MY NAME IF NEED BE — MY MIND FEELS LIKE THE SKY THAT LOOKS DOWN ON EARTH THRIVING WITH STUPENDOUS ECLAT BELOW — I RETREAT TO MY BREATH — EARTH CONTAINS ME IN HER SHELL — I DREAM THE EARTH DREAM IN WHICH EARTH SHOUTS HOSANNAH — THEN THERE IS BRIGHT RINGING SILENCE & I AM THE SILENCE — BUT NOW I HEAR A SOUND THAT APPROACHES — IT IS NOT ANIMAL — IT IS NOT WIND — IT IS NO SOUND EARTH MAKES — IT APPROACHES IN A CLOUD OF DUST & STOPS NOT FAR FROM ME — NOISEMAKER EMERGES TO SIGHT AS DUST SETTLES — IT IS A CRUDE IMITATION OF A SHINY BEETLE — INSTEAD OF LEGS IT HAS WHEELS — IT EXHALES A SMOKE THAT SPOILS THE AIR — IT SEES ME & MOVES TOWARD ME — IT STOPS JUST SHORT OF ME & A CREATURE STEPS OUT — THE CREATURE HAS THE ASPECT OF A MALE ANIMAL BUT I CANNOT BE SURE FOR IT IS COVERED FROM FEET UP TO THE NECK WITH AN ODD NONFUR —

I LOOK INTO THE EYES — I FEEL A SHOCK OF RECOGNITION — THE CREATURE IS MY KIND — I STEP OUT INTO THE OPEN SHOWING THE PALMS OF MY HANDS & I CALL OUT MY NAME — HE APPROACHES WITH THE CORNERS OF HIS MOUTH TURNED UP — HE HOLDS OUT AN OFFERING THAT GLITTERS IN THE SUN — I AM BLINDED BY THE GLITTER — HE GRABS ME & BINDS ME UP & THROWS ME ON A BED THAT'S TOO SHORT FOR ME — HE DRAWS A SWORD & CHOPS OFF MY FEET SO I FIT THE BED — MY DISSEVERED FEET FALL TO THE GROUND AT THE END OF THE BED & MY STUMPS GUSH BLOOD — IT IS GHASTLY & ENTHRALLING

KARMA LOLLIPOP

WHITEMAN CENTRAL BREAK DOWN — THINGS START TO WOBBLE & FALL APART — GLASS SHATTERS METAL CORRODES FERROCONCRETE WEATHERS & CRUMBLES — WHITEMAN CENTRAL BECOMES POOR — DIRT POOR — MORE POOR THAN A 3RD WORLD COUNTRY — SO POOR IT CAN'T EVEN SUPPORT A WEALTHY CLASS — WHITEMAN RETURNS TO HUNTER FORAGER MODE — WHITEMAN'S LAND BECOMES TERRA INCOGNITA — THEN ONE DAY INTO THIS NOT NECESSARILY UNHAPPY SITUATION IN WHICH HARDLY ANYTHING IS HAPPENING BUT LIFE THERE COMES NOVELTY — 1ST IT'S THEIR MISSIONARIES — THEY ARE NOT WHITE — THEY ARE ELFIN & YELLOW — THEY HAVE HIGH CHEEKBONES SLANT EYES & BLACK HAIR — THEY SAY THEY ARE FROM AN ADVANCED HYPERTECH CIVILIZATION ACROSS THE GREAT WATER TO THE WEST IN THE DIRECTION OF THE SETTING SUN & THEY POINT IN THAT DIRECTION SO WHITEMAN

UNDERSTAND — THEY TALK LOUD — THEY SAY WHITEMAN OUR BURDEN — THEY SAY BUDDHA LOVE WHITEMAN EVEN IF WHITEMAN BACKWARD DIRTY & HEATHENISH — THEY WANT WHITEMAN TO CLEAN UP & PUT ON CLOTHES — THEIR TRIP SEEMS TO BE BUDDHA LOVES YOU SANITATION & DON'T LET NUTHIN HANG OUT — SO BIG DEAL IF THAT'S ALL THEY WANT — BUT THEY BROUGHT THE KONG HONG FLU — LESS SAID ABOUT IT THE BETTER — THEN COME THE SOCIAL SCIENTISTS — THEY ARE FROM ANOTHER ADVANCED TECHNOCIVILIZATION OF SMALL BROWN PEOPLE WHERE ALTERED NEURONAL TISSUE CULTURED ON SEWER SLUDGE GROW INTO GIANT BRAINS THAT RUN EVERYTHING — ORGANIC BIOTECH TO THE MAX OR NOTHING — A MARVEL OF THE NEW GOOK SCIENTIFIC IMAGINATION — THEY SAY HEY WHITEMAN YOU DON'T MIND IF WE SET UP OUR CAMP IN YOUR YARD DO YOU — WE WANT TO STUDY YOU — YOU'RE VERY INTERESTING TO US — HEY WHAT'S THAT TOOL YOU GOT IN YOUR HAND — LOOK

FELLAS IT'S AN ARCHAIC VICE GRIP — WE WANT THAT — THEY GIVE WHITEMAN A MESS OF CHEAP BEADS & A TIN MIRROR & THEY TAKE HIS VICE GRIP — AND THEY LEAVE THE YELLOW YAW YAWS — ALMOST 100% MORTALITY FOR WHITEMAN ON THAT ONE — CLOSE — THE YELLOW YAW YAWS ARE LIKE THE HEARTBREAK OF PSORIASIS ONLY MUCH MUCH WORSE — AGAIN LESS SAID ABOUT IT THE BETTER — THEN COME THE POWER & BUCKS PEOPLE — THEY ARE SHORT WITH BROAD FLAT FACES & PERFECT ALMOND EYES YOU'D DIE FOR — THEY DON'T GIVE A SHIT FOR NUTHIN BUT POWER & BUCKS — DERE DA GUYS WHO GOT THE VAPORIZOR GUNS — YOU GET IN THEIR WAY THEY POINT THE VAPORIZOR AT YOU & PULL THE TRIGGER — WHEN THE FORCE HITS IT TURNS YOU INTO A PUFF OF INNOCUOUS VAPOR — NO GORY CORPSE — MAYHEM MADE SANITARY — A GIANT STEP FORWARD FOR CIVILIZATION — A MARVEL OF THE MONGOL SCIENTIFIC IMAGINATION WITH ITS SURREAL MATHEMATIC TURNS FLESH TO VAPOR

— NOW BEFORE THE VERY EYES OF WHITEMAN THESE ADVANCED NONWHITE NATIONS ARE DIVIDING UP WHITEMAN'S LAND INTO WHAT THEY CALL SPHERES OF INFLUENCE — THEY ARE GOING TO PUT A GRID ON WHITEMAN'S LAND & SELL IT OFF DIRT CHEAP FOR KIWI PLANTATIONS WITH WHITEMAN DOING THE GRUNTWORK — THEN ONCE THE PLANTATIONS ARE IN THEY AUTOMATE PLANTATIONS — NOW WHITEMAN ON THE DOLE & REALLY BEGINNING TO GET IN THE WAY OF PROGRESS — SO THESE SUPERTECH NATIONS ROUND UP WHITEMAN THAT IS THE REMNANT POPULATIONS OF WHITEMAN STILL SCATTERED HERE & THERE & THEY PUT THEM INTO WHAT THEY CALL RELOCATION CENTERS THAT CAN MEAN ANYTHING OR NOTHING LIKE RESERVATIONS — NOW THESE NONWHITE ADVANCED MEGATECH NATIONS BEGIN FIGHTING AMONG THEMSELVES — INEVITABLY — ALL POLITICS IS BULLSHIT — THEY MAKE WHITEMAN'S LAND INTO A BATTLEGROUND FOR THEIR WARS — THESE WARS HAVE NOTHING TO

DO WITH WHITEMAN BUT THEY ARE TRASHING
HIS LAND — MEANTIME AMIDST ALL THE CHAOS
OF THIS MOTHER OF ALL WARS ONLY THE
MENEHUNES OF THE WORLD REMAIN CLEAR
CENTERED ON TIME NEUTRAL EACH A VERITABLE
SWITZERLAND OF THE UNIVERSAL POETIC
GENIUS

NOTE
ACCORDING TO HAWAIIAN LEGEND MENEHUNES
ARE SMALL DARK PEOPLE RARELY SEEN WHO
COME OUT AT NIGHT & DO GOOD WORKS THEN
DISAPPEAR BEFORE DAWN

...IVILIZATION IS THE ARTIFAC...
~~NOTHING ELSE~~ OF ^ONE SPECI...
...F ANIMAL GONE ^TOTALLY PSYCHOTI...
SYCHOTIC ^AS DEFINED BY ~~A~~ THE CLINIC~~AL S~~...
^EING NAPPROPRIATE RESPONSE TO S...

...MUST BE APOSTATE FROM...
ECAUSE I BELIEVE ~~HUMAN~~ ^WE...
...A TRIP SO ~~FAR OUT~~ ^STRANGE, THA...
...D WE NOT HAVE A NAME F...
T, LIKE, NORMAL, WE WOUL...
...L, IMMEDIATELY, GO INTO...
TARK RAVING MODE OF...

...MUST BE APOSTATE FROM HUM...
ECAUSE ~~IT LOOKS~~ TO M...
...IVILIZATION IS BASED ON...
NVIDIOUS DISTINCTIONS W...
E ARE SAME WHERE IT
^CIVILIZATION ALWAYS EQUATES AVERAGE WITH N
OUNTS. CIVILIZATION
ONSISTENTLY FAILS TO
DELIVER THE COMMON GOOD
EQUALLY. AND NOW SCIENTI...
IVILIZATION BRINGS ^OUT ALL THE
WORST ~~~~ IN CIVILIZATI...
IT EXAGGERATES OUR PSYC...
PRESENCE OVER EARTH LIK...
SPECTOR ^OF THE ~~IS~~ BROKEN

MUST BE APOSTATE FROM
MAN BECAUSE I BELIEVE
ERE IS NOT ONE THING WE DO GOOD.
T ONE THING. WE'RE FUCKED.
ST WE FUCK OVER OURSELVES
EN WE TURN
CK OVER OUR SURROUND. ON
BUT WE DO PUSH THE BUTTON, S
Y OR THE OTHER YOU BET, AND
D YOU BETTER BELIEVE IT
E BIG SUCKER.. FORSURE WE SUCK.

MUST BE APOSTATE FROM HUMAN
CAUSE I BELIEVE WHAT WE CALL
BELIEVE THE COURSE
CIVILIZATION, THIS RIVER
SLUDGE THROUGH A BLASTED
NDSCAPE, HAS DONE NOTHIN
T REDUCE US TO THIS BLAND
VICIOUS ANIMALS WHO SUCK
WE DO PUSH THE BUTTON GOOD,

UST BE APOSTATE FROM HUMAN
AUSE I BELIEVE THE HUMAN RA
HUMAN E IS APOSTATE
AN EVERY MEMBER OF IT, IS A
E GONE TOTALLY PSYCHOTIC,
HO TIC IN THE CLINICAL SENSE
TO INAPPROPRIATE RESPONSE
I BELIEVE THE

NO SHIT

ECO MOVEMENT IS PURITANISM APPLIED TO NATURE — IT'S EUROCENTRIC IN ITS MISSIONARY ZEAL — FORMERLY XTIAN NOW SCIENTIFIC — MORE OF EUROCENTRAL TELLING NATIVES HEY YOUR WAY NO GOOD ANYMORE CATCH ON WE GOT THE ANSWER — NO SHIT YOU GOT THE ANSWER — & IN THE DEEP ALOHA OF THE NATIVE NOT ADDING IF YOU GOT THE ANSWER HOW COME YOUR OWN PLACE IS IN SUCH AWFUL FUCKING SHAPE — NEVER MIND TRUST US WE KNOW BETTER THAN YOU WHATS GOOD FOR BIOME THAT MEANS ALSO WHATS GOOD FOR YOU — NO SHIT

I MUST BE APOSTATE FROM HUMAN

I MUST BE APOSTATE FROM HUMAN BECAUSE I BELIEVE THERE IS NOT ONE THING WE DO GOOD — NOT ONE THING — WE'RE FUCKED — FIRST WE FUCK OVER OURSELVES THEN WE TURN & FUCK OVER OUR SURROUND — ONE WAY OR THE OTHER — BUT WE DO PUSH THE BUTTON GOOD — I MUST BE APOSTATE FROM HUMAN BECAUSE I BELIEVE WHAT WE CALL THE COURSE OF CIVILIZATION THIS RIVER OF SLUDGE THROUGH A BLASTED LANDSCAPE HAS DONE NOTHING BUT REDUCE US TO BLAND VICIOUS ANIMALS WHO SUCK — YOU BET AND THANKS AND YOU BETTER BELIEVE IT US IS ONE BIG SUCKER — FOR SURE WE SUCK — I MUST BE APOSTATE FROM HUMAN BECAUSE I BELIEVE THE HUMAN RACE INDIVIDUALLY & IN AGGREGATE IS A RACE GONE TOTALLY PSYCHOTIC AND I BELIEVE THE LEADING SYMPTOM OF THIS ABERRANT CONDITION IS WHAT WE CALL CIVILIZATION — THIS MASSIVE HEDGE AGAINST THE TAO OF THE

UNIVERSE — CIVILIZATION IS THE SKEWED ARTIFACT OF ONE SPECIES OF ANIMAL GONE TOTALLY PSYCHOTIC — PSYCHOTIC AS DEFINED BY THE CLINIC — PATIENT EVINCING INAPPROPRIATE RESPONSE TO SURROUND — I MUST BE APOSTATE FROM HUMAN BECAUSE I BELIEVE WE HUMANS ARE ON A TRIP SO FAR OUT THAT DID WE NOT HAVE A NAME FOR IT LIKE NORMAL WE WOULD ALL IMMEDIATELY GO INTO THE STARK RAVING MODE OF IT — I MUST BE APOSTATE FROM HUMAN BECAUSE IT LOOKS TO ME LIKE CIVILIZATION IS BASED ON INVIDIOUS DISTINCTIONS WHEN WE ARE SAME WHERE IT COUNTS — CIVILIZATION CONSISTENTLY FAILS TO DELIVER COMMON GOOD EQUALLY — AND NOW SCIENTIFIC CIVILIZATION BRINGS OUT ALL THE WORST IN CIVILIZATION — IT EXAGGERATES OUR PSYCHOTIC PRESENCE OVER THE EARTH LIKE A SPECTER OF BROCKEN

VOG of KONA MAKES PUNA
LIKE LA SUN
HOT CLOUDS AT ALL LEVELS
MILKY AT EVEN ZENITH AT HORIZON SKY IS STAINLESS STEEL SILVER
AIR UNSTABLE GRAY WITH A TINGE OF PINK — FEELS LIKE STORM
FROM SOUTHWARD
BOUGAINVILLEA LOVES IT —
EVEN WITH THE VOG —
WHICH IS NOTHING COMPARED
TO LA SMOG — THIS
WOULD BE A LIGHT DAY
IN LA OR EAST BAY — NORTHERN CA
GETS
SF's SMOG EVERY DAY PUSHED
OVER BY STRONG WESTERLIES
OFF PACIFIC — TODAY LOOKS
VERANDA BOTH MAUNA KEA &
MAUNA LOA OBSCURED BY V
(LESSER GOLDEN PLOVER)
KOLEA'S ONE TO
SIBERIA
N ALASKA — KOLEA LIKES OUR DIRT
OR SUMMER TO BREED — I'D MISS
NEVER THAT I'VE GOTTEN
A BIRD BUT CLOSE TO THIS
MARVELOUS BIRD OF PASSAGE
WHO THERE — AS I WRITE
THE HOUSE

JUST SHOOK — KILAU
CAP OVER DEEP HAWAII THERM
SPOT CRACKING OOZIN SHAKIN
HAVE HEARD IF YOU CAN FEEL IT IT'S
AT LEAST A 3 ON RICHTER SC
               MANY YRS
BUT WE LIVED
SAN ANDREAS FAULT COUNT
    NORTH COAST OF CALIF
SO WE DON'T FIND EARTHQ
UNSETTLING — WE BEEN
        GRUMBLES ROLL UNDER YO
1ST THE DOG BARKS THEN EARTH
QUAKES WHERE THINGS
            DASH TO FLOOR WITH CLATT
SHELVES   YOU STEP
OFF
OUTSIDE KINDA CRABWISE
    GROUND RIPPLES TREES
SEE 150 DOVE FIRS SHAKIN
WHIPPIN THEIR TOPS LATER YOU HEAR BRICK WALLS CRA
DOWN TO THEIR ROOTS ? IN T
         LIKE THIS JUST
A KONA DAY IS A THE KINDA
DAY EARTHQUAKES LIKE T
HAPPEN   KD'S ARE FULL OF
PORTENT MAKING YOU FEE
LESS SELF WILLED MORE
     YOU UNDERSTAND HAWAIIAN FEELING THAT
     SOUTH WIND IS AN ILL WIND
FATED — A DAY FOR THIN
              NO ESCAPE
CATCH UP WITH YO
          WHEN YOU WAKE UP

BODHISATTVA VOWS

BODHISATTVA VOWS TO BE THE LAST ONE OFF THE SINKING SHIP — YOU SIGN UP & FIND OUT IT'S FOREVER — PASSENGER LIST ENDLESS — SHIP NEVER EMPTIES — SHIP KEEPS SINKING BUT DOESN'T GO QUITE UNDER — ON BOARD ANGST PANIC & DESPERATION HOLD SWAY — TURNS OUT BODHISATTVAHOOD IS A FUCKING JOB LIKE ANY OTHER BUT DIFFERENT IN THAT THERE'S NO WEEKENDS HOLIDAYS VACATIONS NO GOLDEN YEARS OF RETIREMENT — YOU'RE SPENDING ALL YOUR TIME & ENERGY GETTING OTHER PEOPLE OFF THE SINKING SHIP INTO LIFEBOATS BOUND GAILY FOR NIRVANA WHILE THERE YOU ARE SINKING — & OF COURSE YOU HAD TO GO & GIVE YOUR LIFEJACKET AWAY — SO NOW LET US BE CHEERFUL AS WE SINK — OUR SPIRIT EVER BUOYANT AS WE SINK

NUMBNUT

GO INTO TOWN GET ENTIRE TOM CASTRATED — THE GUY IS WITH US 8 YEARS VOLUNTARILY — FELIS CATUS FELL IN WITH US — THEY KNOW OUR TRIP — SO THEY WILL BE ALTERED IF OUR SITUATION DEMANDS IT — SO — MARCEL — MARCELLO — DEAR NUMBNUT — PUS HEAD — JELLO GUY — YOU'VE HAD 8 YEARS OF ABUNDANT PUSSY & FIGHTING — LOOK AT YOUR SCARRED UP FACE — YOUR TATTERED & SHREDDED EARS — YOUR SIDEWISE PUNCHY WALK — TIME TO HANG UP THE GLOVES GUY — YOU WAIT & SEE IT WILL BE A RELIEF — THEY WILL STILL SASHAY BY WITH A GLANCE BACKWARD — YOU WILL STILL SMELL EM AS THEY PASS — YOU WILL SEE & SMELL — YOU WILL REMEMBER — BUT NO MORE WARM RUSH — YOU'RE DEAD DOWN THERE NOW AND JUST AS WELL YOU'LL THINK — I'VE HAD ENUFF PETIT MORT NOW I PREPARE FOR BIG MORT — YOU GOT THE FUCKING LESSON — YOU'LL THINK VACATE ET VIDETE — BE EMPTY & SEE NOW

MONKEY SEE MONKEY DO

LOOK IN PONGID VISIONARY FACE — WE ARE WHO THEY DREAMT OF BEING ONCE — WHAT DO PONGIDS DO BETWEEN ITCHIN & SCRATCHIN — OUR DIRECT ANCESTOR IS A PONGID WHO ONE DAY SAW THE COSMIC ARCHETYPE SHINING CITY — SO WE HAVE OUR SHINING CITY — LOOK IN OUR EYE — WE SEE COSMIC ARCHETYPE ANIMAL IN ITS NICHE WITH NO TOOL BUT RECEIVED MINDBODY — SO WE WILL ADVANCE TO THIS TOTIPOTENT NOTHING — FROM THERE WE WILL APPEAR BARELY FAMILIAR

NOBLE SAVAGE

LET US INVENT OUR NOBLE SAVAGE SO WE KNOW ONE WHEN WE SEE ONE — LET US IMAGINE ANEW THE PERFECTION AT THE BEGINNING OF THINGS — NOBLE SAVAGE INNOCENT OF DEATH — NOBLE SAVAGE UNDERSTANDS THE LANGUAGE OF THE OTHER ANIMALS & TALKS TO THEM & LIVES IN DEEP PEACE WITH THEM — NOBLE SAVAGE NO NEED WORK — WITHOUT LABOR NOBLE SAVAGE FEEDS AT ABUNDANT TREE OF LIFE — NOBLE SAVAGE EATS AND IS EATEN IN DEEP PEACE — NOBLE SAVAGE TALKS TO GOD — NOBLE SAVAGE TRAVELS TO GOD NOT JUST IN SPIRIT BUT CARNATE AND WHOLE — THEY TALK AT GOD'S OASIS BENEATH THE IDEAL PALM — THEY TALK IN THE LANGUAGE OF THE ANIMALS BARKING AND TWITTERING — NOBLE SAVAGE NEVER FALL

COLUMBA LIVIA
WITH PEOPLE IN URBAN SETTING

WATCHED ROCK PIGEONS IN OLD TOWN EUREKA BY CONNIE'S IRISH SHOP — THIS PIGEON OF CITIES — A PAIR WALKING DOWN THE SIDEWALK WITH THE PEOPLE OR PERHAPS MORE APTLY STRUTTING DOWN THE SIDEWALK WITH AN AIR OF AH YES WHAT A LOVELY DAY — THEY'RE SO SELF-ASSURED SO FEARLESS — FROM KNOWING THEY CAN FLY FROM ANY DANGER NO DOUBT — PEOPLE PAY THEM NO MIND — TO US THEY ARE JUST PIGEONS & PIGEONS ARE EVERYWHERE — THEY ARE FOR A FACT — ROCK PIGEONS WERE BROUGHT HERE BY FIRST EUROPEAN COLONISTS & NOW LIKE THE EUROPEAN COLONISTS THEY'VE SPREAD OVER ALL THE TEMPERATE PART OF THE NORTH AMERICAN CONTINENT — I WOULD VENTURE TO SAY THEY'RE FOUND WORLDWIDE WHEREVER PEOPLE HAVE TAKEN THEM — BEAUTIFUL PORTABLE CONVENIENT PACKAGE LIVE FRESH MEAT — SHALL IT BE SPLIT BODY BBQ

— BUT MOSTLY WE DON'T EAT EM WE LIVE WITH EM — THEY ARE LIKE A CAT OR DOG OF THE BIRD WORLD TO US — THEY ARE AMONGST US LIKE THE COW IS AMONGST THE HINDU — BUT THEY ARE WILD — AT THE SAME TIME THEY LIKE TO BE WITH US — THEY HANG AROUND US VOLUNTARILY CAN YOU BELIEVE IT — THEY DON'T EVEN MIND OUR MOST CONGESTED URBAN SCENES — LOOK AT EM IN SF UNION SQUARE RIGHT IN THERE WITH THE NOISY RELENTLESS TRAFFIC THE VIRTUAL FLOODS OF PEOPLE THE BAD AIR THE AMALGAM SMELL OF URBAN HUMAN SCENE THE UTTER ECO-DEVASTATION OF MODERN URBAN WHERE RELIEF IS ONLY UPWARD TO BLUE SKY IF YOU CAN SEE IT THROUGH SMOKY DESIRE THERE RIGHT IN THERE IS ROCK PIGEON VOLUNTARILY WITH THE PEEPS — JUST LIKE THE RAT MOUSE & FLY — THIS ANIMAL IS FOR REAL — STRAIGHT SHOT FLIGHT & FLUTTER LANDING — THEY GO GOOD WITH CANARY ISLAND DATE PALMS — THEY ENJOY CITY PARKS EVEN WITHOUT LAWNS — THEY LOVE STONE LEDGES & ROOF EDGES —

THEY LIKE TO PREEN & ARE FASTIDIOUS WHILE THEY SHIT EVERYWHERE — THEY'RE A LOT LIKE US — THEY HAVE FEELINGS OF DECENCY LIKE US TOO AS CONSIDER THE RELATIVELY FEW DEAD PIGEONS YOU SEE ON THE STREETS AS COMPARED TO THEIR NUMBERS LIVE — YOU CAN ONLY CONCLUDE THEY HAVE THE DECENCY TO GO OFF AND DIE OUT OF SIGHT — WE APPRECIATE THIS KIND OF THOUGHTFULNESS — I FOR ONE BELIEVE ALL ANIMALS HAVE THIS INNATE COURTESY SO I THINK WE HAVE NOTHING TO FEAR IF ONE DAY WE ARE JOINED ON OUR SIDEWALKS BY A MOTHER RACCOON WITH HER KITS JUST OUT FOR A STROLL A PAIR OF BLUE HERONS GAZING AT A PEACOCK FEATHER IN A WINDOW A BOBCAT SMELLING PISS AT A FIRE HYDRANT A DOE WITH HER FAWN AT A CORNER WAITING FOR THE LIGHT TO CHANGE A BEAR SITTING ASPRAWL A SUNNY DOORSTEP A FAMILY OF COUNTRY MICE IN TOWN FOR A DAY SHARING A DISH OF ICE CREAM AT THE CURB A SOLITARY PORCUPINE UP ON HIND LEGS LOOKING AT A POTTED BARREL

CACTUS IN A SHOP WINDOW WITH DOGGED CURIOSITY THINKING IT LOOKS LIKE ME ONLY POTTED A PUMA HURRYING TO AN APPOINTMENT A SQUIRREL TURNING OVER A BOTTLE CAP WITH US AMONG THEM YES US AMONG THEM & WE WILL NOT EVEN NOTICE THEM ANY MORE THAN WE NOTICE OUR COMPANION ROCK PIGEONS STRUTTING & PECKING DOWN THE SIDEWALK BESIDE US — WE WILL ONLY JOSTLE EACH OTHER AS WE PASS — ROCK PIGEON LOOKING DOWN ON SCENE FROM ROOF EDGE WILL THINK THEY FINALLY GOT THE IDEA — ALL IS ONE — THIS PIONEER OF INTERSPECIES MUTUALISM

TREES

TREES ARE SO SIMPLE IN THEIR MIGHT — SUCK UP CO_2 GIVE OFF OXYGEN — SUCK UP WATER OUT OF DIRT PUT OUT NEW GREENY LEAVES — TREE SAY GREEN TO LIGHT — TREE TAKE SUN MAKE SUGAR — TREE NO NEED FEET TO WALK — LIKES WHERE IT'S AT — STAY PUT IN WIND AND DANCE IN ONE SPOT — OTHERWISE TREE EVER PATIENT IN ITS HABIT — TREE NO TALK SO NO TREE WARS — SWEET TREE SEX NOT VENEREAL — TREE STAND — TREE THROW COOL SHADE TO GROUND — TREE REACH UP AND DOWN AND SIDEWAYS — TREE BRAVE DON'T FLINCH WHEN CHAIN SAW PUT TO IT — TREE DON'T HAVE RED BLOOD — TREE SAY GO AHEAD KILL ME SEE IF I CARE — ANYWAY TREE GOT PARTY GOING ALL THE TIME — THE BUGS AND THE BIRDS — LICHEN AND FUNGI — MYCORRHIZAE AT THE ROOTS AND UP THE TREE THE SQUIRRELS POSSUMS GRINNING CATS RACCOONS AND OTHER ASSORTED ANIMALS EVEN PORCUPINES BETIMES — LIGHT PLAYS ON

LEAVES — LEAVES SHUDDER — TREE LIKE RAIN WASH OFF MAN DUST IF RAIN NOT ACID — EVEN DEAD TREE MAKE FIRE

A BEAST FABLE

WE BREACH OUT IN SHOALING WATER — WE STEP OUT ON LAND — WE ARE EVERY ANIMAL BUT HOMO SAPIENS — WE HAVE COME TO TAKE EARTH BACK — WE DECLARE THIS LAND FOR STANDARD EARTH WHERE LIFE ABIDES & EVERY CREATURE SHARES COMMON EARTH WEALTH — WE LOOK PAST HUMAN SUNBATHERS WHO PROTEST OUR INVASION OF THEIR PRIVATE MARINA — DON'T PROTEST — YOU KNOW THE LAW OF KARMA — AS YOU DO UNTO OTHERS TO EXACT MEASURE THE SAME IS DONE TO YOU — EXTERMINATION THEN WITHOUT MERCY — WE SEND IN OUR SHOCK TROOPS — YOU CANNOT SEE THEM THOUGH THEY NUMBER IN THE JILLIONS — A SINGLE CELL DYNAMO WHOSE SOUL IS VENGEANCE — SENT DIRECT TO US BY GALACTIC ARCHEOBIO — IT HOMES IN ONLY ON HUMANS — YOU ARE UTTERLY NAIVE TO IT — IT WILL BE VIRGIN SOIL PANDEMIC — UNIVERSAL INFECTION IMPACT — LETHAL — 100% DEATH RATE — ONCE

INFECTION SETS IN DEATH FOLLOWS SWIFT AS AN ORGASM — NOW WE SEND IN THE CREATURES WHO SCAVENGE — THEY CONVERT YOU TO MYRIAD WHITISH TURDS SCATTERED OVER LANDSCAPE — WHITISH BECAUSE THEY CAN EAT & DIGEST BONE — WE MOVE INLAND PAST INTACT REAL ESTATE & PERSONAL PROPERTY — WITHOUT YOU AND STILL THEY HAVE GAINED A PRISTINE QUALITY WITH THE FEEL OF NATURAL OBJECTS — NOW WE ARE EACH AT OUR ANCESTRAL NICHE AGAIN — NOW WE CAN DREAM EXISTENCE AGAIN EACH IN OUR OWN WAY

A KONA

AN APRIL KONA BLOCKS OFF TRADES MAKES PUNA VOGGY LIKE SMOGGY LA — PU'U 'O'O BEEN SMOKIN 8 YRS LONGEST ERUPTION ON RECORD — SUN HOT THRU SCATTERED CLOUDS AT ALL LEVELS — SKY MILKY EVEN AT ZENITH — AT HORIZON SKY IS STAINLESS STEEL SILVER GRAY WITH A TINGE OF PINK TECHNOHAZE — AIR UNSTABLE BLOWING ONE DIRECTION THEN ANOTHER — FEELS LIKE STORM APPROACHING FROM SOUTHWARD — OUR MAGENTA BOUGAINVILLEA LOVES IT — THE HEAT — EVEN WITH THE VOG WHICH IS NUTHING COMPARED TO LA SMOG — THIS WOULD BE A LIGHT DAY IN LA OR EAST BAY NORTHERN CAL THAT GETS SF'S SMOG PUSHED OVER EVERY DAY BY STRONG WESTERLIES OFF PACIFIC — TODAY LOOKING FROM BACK VERANDA BOTH MAUNA KEA & MAUNA LOA OBSCURED BY VOG — KŌLEA GONE TO WEST ALASKA & SIBERIA FOR SUMMER TO BREED — I NEVER THOUGHT I'D MISS A BIRD BUT

I'VE GOTTEN CLOSE TO THIS MARVELOUS BIRD OF PASSAGE — WHOA — THERE — AS I WRITE THE HOUSE JUST SHOOK — KĪLAUEA CAP OVER DEEP HAWAI'I THERMAL SPOT CRACKIN OOZIN SHAKIN — HAVE HEARD IF YOU CAN FEEL IT IT'S AT LEAST A 3 ON RICHTER SCALE — BUT WE LIVED MANY YEARS IN SAN ANDREAS FAULT COUNTRY ALONG NORTH COAST OF CALIF SO WE DON'T FIND EARTHQUAKES UNSETTLING — WE BEEN IN QUAKES WHERE 1ST THE DOG BARKS THEN EARTH RUMBLES & ROLLS UNDER YOU AND THINGS JARRED OFF SHELVES DASH TO FLOOR WITH CLATTER AND YOU STEP OUTSIDE KINDA CRABWISE & SEE GROUND RIPPLING & 150' DOUG FIR TREES WHIPPING THEIR TOPS & SHAKING DOWN TO THEIR ROOTS & LATER YOU HEAR BRICK WALLS CRACKED IN TOWN — A KONA DAY LIKE THIS IS JUST THE KINDA DAY EARTHQUAKES LIKE TO HAPPEN — KONA DAYS ARE FULL OF PORTENT MAKING YOU FEEL LESS SELF-WILLED & MORE FATED — YOU UNDERSTAND HAWAIIAN FEELING THAT SOUTH WIND IS AN ILL WIND — A

DAY FOR THINGS TO CATCH UP WITH YOU AND
NO ESCAPE — UNLESS YOU'RE KŌLEA AND FLY
OFF TO W. ALASKA OR SIBERIA — I BET KŌLEA
BEEN COMING HAWAI'I A LONG TIME EVEN
BEFORE HUMANS GOT HERE — PRE-HUMAN
HAWAI'I THERE'S SOMETHING TO THINK ABOUT
— THE AIR IS SMOKY NOW AS MANY TIMES
BEFORE IN HAWAI'I NEI — LOOKS LIKE IT LOOKS
WHEN YOU'RE ABOUT 100 MILES DOWNWIND
FROM A SMALL FOREST FIRE IN NORTHERN CAL
COASTAL RANGE — NOW — HOLD IT — WIND HAS
SHIFTED AND BECOME A TRADE THAT BENDS
OVER THE LONG-LEGGED RED TI PLANT MAKING
ITS LEAVES WHIP ABOUT AND MAKING BANANA
LEAVES TO FLAP AND FLUTTER — VOG PILING UP
AGAINST THE SADDLE — I CAN SEE BANK OF
MILKY SMOKE MOVING THROUGH TREES IN
DISTANCE — I CAN HEAR DISTANT BIRD CALL AS
FROM ANOTHER EON FAINTLY — THE 'ŌHI'A
BRANCHES SHAKE THEIR LEAVES WITH PATIENCE
AND TAKE THE HYDROGEN SULFIDE — LIFE IS A
VALE OF H_2S ANY WAY YOU PUT IT — NOW THE

WIND HAS STEPPED UP AND I CAN HEAR IT
BLOWING THRU TREES AND AROUND HOUSE —
THE AIR HAS COOLED — CLOUDS BEGIN PILE UP
AGAINST LONG WALL OF FOR ME LOOKING WEST
FROM L TO R MAUNA LOA AT 13,679' THEN LONG
SADDLE PLATEAU AT 6,000' THEN MAUNA KEA
UPTHRUST TO 13,796' — CLOUDS GATHER AND
TURN BLUE-GRAY UNDER AND MERGE INTO ONE
CLOUD OVER PUNA — THE AFTERNOON CLOUD
OVER PUNA — SOME CLOUD — PUNA IS LARGER
THAN O'AHU — WHY IS THE MONGOOSE
CHIRPING IN THE YARD — I WILL BE SURPRISED
IF A FINE MIST DOESN'T BEGIN TO FALL SOON
THEN THE MIST TURN TO A DRIZZLE BY LATE
AFTERNOON AND BY EVENING TO INTERMITTENT
PELTING SHOWERS — I'M THINKING OF KŌLEA ON
50 HR FLIGHT ACROSS GREAT WATER IN SUN AND
STORM 2 DAYS & 2 NITES NONSTOP TO THEIR
SUMMER BREEDING GROUNDS IN W ALASKA &
SIBERIA WHERE THEY HAVE HAD THEIR
BREEDING GROUNDS SINCE PRE-HUMAN TIMES —
BIRDS BEEN AROUND LOTS LOTS LONGER THAN

US — FROM JURASSIC TIMES OUT OF REPTILES — MAYBE THIS FEATHERED REPTILE SENIOR TO US BY 160 MILL YRS CAN TEACH US SOMETHING — LIKE IT'S REPORTED THEY HAVE THIS INTERESTING CUSTOM OF MAINTAINING THEIR FORAGING TERRITORIES DURING THE DAY THEN ABANDONING THESE TERRITORIES AT NIGHT TO GATHER AND ROOST TOGETHER IN FLOCKS — SOME KIND OF ANIMAL CIVILITY HERE — SOME KIND OF POLITIC FOR BEING TOGETHER AND ALONE — HUMANS GOTTA CHANGE THE WAY THEY ARE IN NATURE — THERE IS A PAIR OF KŌLEA WHOSE TERRITORY THE COUNTY TAX MAP LISTS AS OURS — WE WON'T BE SUING KŌLEA OVER THIS — KŌLEA'S PROPRIETARY RIGHT TO THIS PIECE OF EARTH IS MUCH OLDER THAN OURS — I MISS KŌLEA HOP FLYING AHEAD OF CAR THEN AT WIDE SPOT STOPPING ROADSIDE WHILE I PASS SLOWLY WATCHING ME PASS WITH ALERT DETACHED CURIOSITY — THERE — A HARD DRIZZLE MAKING WHITE NOISE ON METAL ROOF — WE HAVE OPEN CEILING WITH EXPOSED

RAFTERS AND PURLINGS SO CAN SEE UNDERSIDE OF METAL ROOF — WE LIVE IN A RAIN DRUM — RAIN FALLS IN PULSES — EACH RAIN HAS A DIFFERENT BEAT — NOT ALL KONA DAYS ARE LIKE THIS — THERE'S A DIFFERENT KIND OF KONA — THESE OTHER KONAS ARE AS CLOSE AS YOU CAN GET TO PERFECT WEATHER — ON SUCH A DAY UPLAND PUNA DAWNS CLOUDLESS CLEAR — THE WIND IS FROM SW BLOWING VOG OUT TO SEA THEN CURLING IT UP TOWARD HĀMĀKUA AND ON TO MAUI, OʻAHU AND BEYOND — ON SUCH A DAY THE WEATHER IS OPEN AND NATURE APPEARS IN ALL ITS FRANKNESS AND BEAUTY — STEPPING OUT OF THE HOUSE INTO THE YARD ON SUCH A DAY IS LIKE BREAKING THROUGH GRAMMAR TO SENSE — THE SKY IS HARD BRIGHT BLUE — THE SUN IS A BRILLIANT BALL YOU DO NOT LOOK AT BUT FEEL AS DRY RELAXING HEAT THAT PENETRATES TO BONE — YOU THINK YOU'RE KONA SIDE — YOU FEEL LEEWARD — IT FEELS LIKE PRE-WWII SOUTHERN CALIFORNIA USED TO FEEL — ON SUCH A DAY WITH THE

SLIGHTEST EXERTION YOU BREAK OUT IN A FINE SWEAT THAT ZEPHYROUS S WESTERLY COOLS OFF YOU — BEAUTEOUS INSULAR YOU SAY — NOW COME THE FIRST PELTING SHOWERS — SOUND OF WATER FALLING ON ROOF LAVES THE SPIRIT — SEVERAL WEEKS AGO SAW MALE KŌLEA IN ITS BREEDING DRESS ALREADY WITH DASHING WHITE BAND ACROSS FOREHEAD OVER EYE AND DOWN SIDES OF NECK AND I THOT SO THEY'LL BE GONE SOON AND WITHIN A WEEK THEY WERE GONE TO W ALASKA AND SIBERIA — GONE LIKE KONAS WHEN TRADES KICK BACK IN — GONE TO COME BACK

SUMMER SOLSTICE

1

PETROLIA

LAST DAY OF SPRING TAKE WALK ON BEACH — COLD STRONG WIND OFF OCEAN MAKE SAND DANCE — THE THREE OF US — ME HER AND WHITE SHE DOG — WE WALK TO WHERE THE RIVER FLOWS INTO OCEAN — BEACH FLOWERS IN BLOOM — THE STICKY SAND-VERBENA WITH NEAT YELLOW CLUSTERS IN FULL FLOWER — THE ROSE PINK BEACH MORNING GLORY — THE YELLOW BEACH EVENING PRIMROSE OENOTHERA — THE BEACH MUSTARD CAKILE ONE WHITE ONE VIOLET — SKY OVERHEAD CLEAR BLUE AND SPACEY — RIVER WATER CLEAR AND AQUAMARINE WHERE IT RUNS OVER WHITE SAND — AS RIVER HIT ELEVATED STRAND AT BEACH IT WORE OUT A CURVE OF BANK THAT TURNED IT SHARPLY TO ONE SIDE AND SHOT IT BACKWARD AGAINST ANOTHER BANK CURVING IT IN TURN

— A MEANDER BUILT IN SAND AT END OF RIVER RUN — ITS LAST SIGNATURE AN S — IN THIS LAST SHORT MEANDER IT RAN OVER A BED OF ROUNDED STONES AND BOULDERS THAT MADE WATER LILT AND BOUNCE IN GAY WAVELETS WITH SPARKLY LEAPING LACY CAPS — AND IT WENT THAT WAY TO THE FIRST THIN LINE OF WHITE SURF WHERE IT PASSED BACK INTO MOTHER PANTHALASSA

2

MANILA ON ARCATA BAY

NEXT DAY ANOTHER BEACH 60 MILES UP COAST — SOLSTICE PARTY — IS IT FOR CELEBRATING THE FACT THAT OUR DAYS WILL BE GETTING SHORTER NOW — JERRY'S HOUSE AND DUNE MARSH OR SANDBAR LAGOON WITH WILLOWS — LAST HOUSE ON ROAD UP A SAND DUNE RISE — LAST HOUSE ON ROAD IS WHERE TO BE — THE OCEAN WAS SOUNDING STRONGLY OTHER SIDE OF LAST DUNES — FAST MASSIVE MOVEMENT OF COOL AIR

TO HOT INLAND BLEW HARD CHARGING UP THE AIR — A BLUE HERON WITH WIDESPREAD WINGS ROSE OUT OF LAGOON AGAINST THE WIND — PEOPLE GATHERED TO THE HOUSE — THEY PRESSED AGAINST THE HOUSE ON THE PORCH ON BENCHES AND STEPS — WITH THE PEOPLE CAME VARIETIES OF GRUB DRINKS AND JOINTS — A FIRE WAS LIT IN A NEAR RUSTED OUT ORANGY-BROWN WITH RUST BBQ OVEN FROM THE LATE 20TH CENTURY — GRILLED KEBABS AND SALMON DONE RIGHT — OUR EARNEST CHATTER OUR MURMURS & LAUGHTER ROSE IN THE AIR AND WERE SWEPT TO SOUTHEASTWARD BY THE WIND OVER ARCATA BAY AND BEYOND FAR BEYOND — OUR WORDS THAT SAY EMBRACE ME I'M SINKING — I WENT TO THE SIDE OF THE HOUSE TO PISS — ON LAGOON FEMALE MALLARD PADDLED INTO DEEP SHADE OF WILLOWS SHOWING BRIGHT BLUE SPECULUM AT WING — AT SIDE OF HOUSE AN OLD SQUARE BLOCK OF CONCRETE STUCK NEXT TO THE FOUNDATION — IT IS NOW PERFECTLY CURED AT 50 YEARS OR MORE I ESTIMATE —

STAINED BROWN LIKE A CHUNK OF FAUX WOOD — THE BRICKS OF THE FIREPLACE THAT ONCE SAT ON THIS CONCRETE BLOCK TURN UP HERE AND THERE IN THE YARD LOOKING LIKE RUINS IN A ROMANTIC PAINTING IN THE LATE AFTERNOON LIGHT OF THIS LONGEST DAY OF THE YEAR — TO THE FRONT OF THE HOUSE THE PALM-LIKE CORDYLINE TOSSED ITS HEAD OF LANCEOLATE LEAVES IN THE WIND — BENEATH IT I SAT ON A BENCH AT THE SIDE OF A BRICK WALK LAID DOWN BY SOME ED & DONNA IN AN ALL TOO IRRETRIEVABLE PAST — THEIR NAMES SCRATCHED INTO A PATCH OF CONCRETE AT THE FRONT EDGE OF THE WALK — SITTING THERE I HEARD OF A MASSIVE CORONARY — THE BRICKS HAVE AGED TO A WARM TERRA COTTA — THEY LEAD TO THE STEPS OF THE PORCH — THE PORCH IS NOW CROWDED WITH PEOPLE — SOME COLLECTION OF NORTH COAST LITERATI — HAVE I HEARD THE SPIRIT RISES AS THE WHISKEY WARMS — I OVERHEAR A GROUP OF WOMEN TALKING ABOUT MEN IN THEIR PAST & PRESENT

— ONE SEZ AND I TOLD HIM YOU WANT YOUR FOOD FAST THEN GO DOWN TO MCDONALD'S AND GET YOUR FAST FOOD AND WHILE YOU'RE THERE BRING ME BACK A BIG MAC WILLYA — THEY LAUGH AGAINST THE WIND — THE INSIDE OF THE HOUSE IS NEAT — AN INTERIOR ALWAYS LOOKS GOOD WHEN IT'S BEING WORKED ON AND YOU CAN SEE THE BONES OF THE HOUSE — NARROW LONG HOUSE TWO STORIES — FLOOR HIGH ALONG CENTER LENGTH AND SLOPING DOWN EVENLY TO BOTH SIDE WALLS — WHO NEEDS A PERFECTLY LEVEL FLOOR — WINDOWS LOOK OUT TO DUNES — SEVEN YEARS ON THE LAM SEZ THIS DUDE THEN I GAVE MYSELF UP — OUT OF SOUTH WINDOW DUNES WITH A FEW SNAGS RISING OUT OF DUNES LIKE THE POTTERY HAND WITH SPREAD FINGERS REACHING FROM OUT OF FLOWER PLOT BELOW THE PORCH — A CONTRIBUTION FROM THE HOUSE'S FORMER RESIDENT A POTTER — FROM INSIDE THE HOUSE I HEAR A VOICE OUTSIDE PROCLAIM I'M TRISEXUAL — ON THE SOUTH WALL A PAINTING

BY JOY DELLAS OF BLUE SKY ABOVE PINKISH BUMPY MAMMARY DUNES OUT OF WHICH RISE THOSE BLACK SNAGS OF FIR OR CYPRESS WITH HOUSETOPS BUMPY TREE CROWNS & TELEPHONE POLES ALONG THE BOTTOM — THEN AS THE LIGHT OF DAY DECLINED WE THOUGHT OF HOME AND THE ANIMALS WAITING — WE LEFT THE PARTY — A PARTY THAT WAS PROOF GOOD TIMES ARE ALWAYS WITH US ALL INDICATIONS TO THE CONTRARY NOTWITHSTANDING — WE STARTED HOME SOUTH ALONG THE FLAT LEVEL DARKENING BAY WITH GAY WAVELETS ON IT MOVING IN THE SAME DIRECTION WE WERE GOING

IF NOT CIVILIZATION THEN WHAT

I WANT 2 SIDES OF BRAIN EQUAL SIZE & IN PERFECT SYNC DELIVERING ME THE WORLD APE ANCESTOR DREAMT OF & NOT THIS RIGHT HANDED AD HYPE DREAMTIME — I WANT MY GOLDEN AGE — I WANT DEVOTION NOT SYSTEMS OF PROMOTION — ANIMAL DEVOTION — THE QUIET OF THE SNAKE — THE MEAN LIFE EXPECTANCY OF MEDIEVAL CISTERCIAN MONK WAS 28 — SAY THEY ENTERED ORDER IN MID TO LATE TEENS — THEY HAD ON AVERAGE JUST A DOZEN YEARS TO BREAK THROUGH TO FLOWER OF DEATH SUCH WAS THE PHYSICAL PRIVATION TRIP OF THE ORDER THEN — THEY COULD LAST JUST THAT LONG ON ROOTS OATCAKES HARD PHYSICAL LABOR & POVERTY OF THE KIND THEY PUT ON THEMSELVES — HERE'S ANIMAL DEVOTION — THEY UNDERSTOOD BODY IS ALLEGORY — THEY ALLOWED THEMSELVES TWO BEAUTIES — CHANTED ORISON & SMOOTH HEWN STONE — THEY MADE EVERYTHING OF STONE —

THIS WAS NOT CIVILIZATION — IT WAS THE DIVINE ARCHITECTURE OF THE HIVE — I WANT RAPTURE FOR MY NATURAL STATE — I WANT TO STAND FORTH IN BLAKEAN NAKEDNESS WITH UNIVERSAL CELESTIAL ALMANAC HARDWIRED INTO BRAIN SO CAN TRAVEL TO ANY POINT IN TIME LIKE SPACE & RETURN — I WANT TO NEED NO TOOL — I WANT TO GO TO AT LEAST HEXACHROMATIC VISION WHERE AIR BECOMES SO TEXTURED I CAN MOUNT IT LIKE A BIRD — I WANT TO PIONEER THIS GOLDEN AGE OF HEXACHROMATIC VISION — & AS I ROAM OVER EARTH SHOULD I HIT ARCTIC WEATHER I WANT POWER OF METABOLIC ARREST SO CAN FREEZE METABOLISM TO 1% OF NORMOTHERMIC RATE LIKE SOME FROGS INSECTS & OTHER ANIMALS CAN DO SO I FREEZE TO CRYSTALLINE STATE & RESIDE IN CRYSTAL CAGE AS LIQUID LIGHT HELD BY CONSTANT BEAUTIES OF CRYSTALLINE SHIFT TILL WARMTH RETURNS TO THAW ME OUT — OR IF I HIT SUFFOCATING DRYING HEAT I WANT POWER OF METABOLIC ARREST TO REDUCE ME

TO A DRY CYST AT EXTREME LIMIT OF DESSICATION TO WAIT FOR RAIN — AND I WANT SOLITARY RATHER THAN GREGARIOUS FOR WHAT WE CALL HISTORY IS OVERWHELMING PROOF THAT GREGARIOUS WITH PERPETUAL SEXUAL RECEPTIVITY HAS BEEN A DISASTROUS STRATEGY FOR HUMAN — I WANT TO BE SOLITARY & EAT AT COMMON TABLE OF EARTH WITHOUT BENEFITING OR HARMING ANYONE — THE CIVILIZED STATE ALWAYS CAUSES US TO WANT UTOPIA — BUT THERE IS NO UTOPIA WITHOUT UTOPIC MIND — UTOPIC MIND CAN'T EXIST IN CIVILIZATION BECAUSE UTOPIC MIND IS FREE OF THEORY & CIVILIZATION IS NOTHING ELSE — THE GOLDEN AGE CAN'T BE DESIGNED FROM OUTSIDE — IT MUST HAPPEN LIKE DAWN OR DARWIN'S FINCHES

(53 FINGERS)
TO MICHAEL WENGER

FORM EMPTY
READING THE HEART SUTRA AGAIN AFTER MANY YEARS

1

IF FORM IS EMPTY —
EMPTY FORM — IF THEY
ARE ONE & THE SAME
THING — ~~FORM EMPTY~~
WHY DOES IT TAKE 2 WORDS
PARADOXIC TO EXPRESS ITS
IN STATEMENT THAT IN PLAIN
SPECIAL WORDS LANGUAGE ARE
CONTRADICTORY — FORM
IN THE FACE OF IT IS NOT HOW CAN EMPTY HAVE FOR
THIS PARADOXICAL EMPTY — WHY
SYMBOLIC INSTEAD OF
STATEMENT SIMPLE WORD FOR IT —
OF A SINGLE WORD FOR SUN
LIKE THE WORD SUN

2
FIRST — (NOT IRONIC
WHY — A BECUZ LIFE IS A PARADOX
LIVING IS FILLED WITH IRONY (UNLIKE THE SUN WHICH IS)
WAY — IT IS TOO IMPROBABLE LIFE WON'T BE EXPRESSED IN
SECOND QUALITY — BECUZ THERE
IS NO OTHER WAY TO SAY IT THAT
EXPRESSES THE DEEP PATHOS
OF SPIRIT INCARNATE — LIKE PATHOS YOU
GOT A STICK I'LL GIVE YOU A STICK YOU
DON'T HAVE A STICK I'LL TAKE IT
AWAY — IRONIC LIKE THE ANSWER
DOESN'T MATCH THE QUESTION

BUT A SPECIES OF UNIV

COULD SEE THEN
LIVING & DYING WERE BUT TERMS
           MAMA, DID YOU CALL?
I BELIEVE THAT AT A CERTAIN
IN STAR SYSTEM OUT OF MOTHERLIGHT THERE IS A
    STAR FORMATION, PSYCHIC KNOTS
OF MIRIAD UNITS OF ZERO MASS, LET'S CALL THEM, SOU
INTO TIME LIKE SPACE, LIKE ALL ENT
IMPROBABLE STATE PSYCHIC IMPROBABILITY IS A STRESSFUL STATE
           SOUL ENDURES PAIN O
IMPROBABLE STATE   TIME LIFESPAN SEEKS A VEH
           PUSHED THROUGH BY SOUL RADIATION ITS POINT EARTH
EXPRESSING THIS PAIN IN A GRAPHIC N
UNIVERSE IS A STATION WHET
WHO SUFFER IN A BROADLY SIMIL
CONGREGATE SOULS MINERAL VEGETAB
EACH CALLING OUT ITS NAME IS WHAT WE COMPRE
    AS OUR EARTH WORLD.
THE COURSE OF SOUL IS   IS
           THRU BIRTHS & DEATHS
                   BIRTH WAKE STATE
           BIRTH LIVING DYING BARDO BIRTH LIVIN
           BIRTH IS DEATH — DEATH IS BIRTH
PREFERABLE TO DEATH
EACH STATE AS REAL AS THE OTHER
               (LIKE A PARTICLE OR WAVE ARE THE SA
           IN FACT THE SAME) A KNOT
                   BIRTH IS DEATH DEATH IS
UNRAVEL, RELAX & DISAPPEAR FINALLY.
SAME TIME EVERY ENTITY WANTS
                        HERE'S A RECIPE FOR
PERPETUATE ITS IDENTITY.   SUFFER
           OF SOUL'S WAVE LIKE COU
AT EACH PEAK & TROUGH   MOT
LIGHT APPEARS & CALLS TO
           BUT SOULS BECOME ENGROSSED IN THEIR PA
SOUL TO COME HOME NOW, B
           HEARS CLEARLY &
SOUL FINALLY GOES HOME
           DISAPPEARS INTO MOTHE

FORM EMPTY
READING THE HEART SUTRA AGAIN AFTER MANY YEARS

1

IF FORM IS EMPTY AND EMPTY FORM — IF THEY ARE ONE & THE SAME — WHY DOES IT TAKE 2 WORDS IN A PARADOXIC STATEMENT TO EXPRESS IT — 2 WORDS THAT IN PLAIN LANGUAGE ARE CONTRADICTORY — FORM ON THE FACE OF IT IS NOT EMPTY & HOW CAN EMPTY HAVE FORM — WHY THIS PARADOXICAL OXYMORONIC STATEMENT INSTEAD OF A SINGLE SIMPLE WORD FOR IT— LIKE THE WORD SUN FOR SUN

2

WHY — FIRST — BECUZ UNLIKE THE SUN WHICH IS NOT IRONIC LIFE IS A PARADOX AND LIVING IS FILLED WITH IRONY — LIFE WON'T BE EXPRESSED IN ANY PAT WAY — IT IS TOO IMPROBABLE — & — SECOND — BECUZ THERE IS NO OTHER WAY TO SAY IT THAT EXPRESSES THE DEEP PATHOS OF

SPIRIT CARNATE — PATHOS LIKE YOU GOT A STICK I'LL GIVE YOU A STICK YOU DON'T HAVE A STICK I'LL TAKE IT AWAY — IRONIC LIKE THE ANSWER DOESN'T MATCH THE QUESTION HOWEVER YOU PUT IT

EYAT

EYAT HAD ONLY 2 SURVIVING SPEAKERS, BOTH OLD, IN THE LATE 1970'S AND MAY NOW BE EXTINCT.
  MERRITT RUHLEN
  A GUIDE TO THE WORLD'S
  LANGUAGES

WE ARE THE LAST ONES TO SPEAK OUR TONGUE — JUST YOU AND I — NO ONE ELSE KNOWS WHAT WE SAY — THE SHAPE OF OUR THOT HAS BECOME OLD AND SECRET — WE HAVE BECOME OLD AND SECRET — OTHERS HEAR US BUT DO NOT UNDERSTAND — THEY LOOK AT US LIKE WE HAVE JUST RETURNED FROM THE DEAD — BUT WE STILL EAT WILD STRAWBERRIES BOILED NETTLE & SMOKED SALMON — WE STILL SIT BY OUR FIRE THO IT SEEMS TO GET SMALLER AND LESS WARM BUT THERE IS LESS TO WARM NOW — LET US SPEAK ALL THE WORDS OF OUR TONGUE ONCE MORE SO IT HAS NO MORE TO SAY — IT WILL BE

LESS THAN A DRY CREEK — LET US WALK OUT NOW AND CALL EACH THING BY ITS NAME AND HEAR IT ANSWER ONE LAST TIME — THEN WE CAN RETURN TO OUR FIRE AND SAY THE LAST WORD TO EACH OTHER

COSMOVISION

THERE'S COSMOS OF CONSCIOUSNESS THAT ALL CREATION SHARES AS A COMMON — THE SUPPORT SYSTEM OF THE PHYSICAL UNIVERSE — REVIVE IDEA OF ETHER (CALL IT COSMOCONSCIOUSNESS) — IT PERVADES UNIVERSE EVENLY IN ALL DIRECTIONS. OBJECTS DO NOT DISPLACE THIS ETHER OF COSMOCONSCIOUSNESS — THE ETHER PERVADES OBJECTS EVENLY AS EVENLY AS IT PERVADES SPACE BETWEEN OBJECTS — IT IS NOT HIGHER IN ONE CREATURE THAN IN ANOTHER — IT IS NO STRONGER INSIDE OUR HEAD THAN IT IS OUTSIDE OUR HEAD — IS IN ALL EQUALLY — IT EXPRESSES DIFFERENT IN EACH THING SO THERE ARE WORLDS & THERE ARE WORLDS — THERE ARE NEITHER HIGHER OR LOWER WORLDS — THERE ARE MERELY DIFFERENT WORLDS — OUR BODY BRAIN IS A DEVISE FOR TRANSLATING COSMOCONSCIOUSNESS INTO EARTH TERMS — WE DO NOT ORIGINATE CONSCIOUSNESS, WE TAP INTO CONSCIOUSNESS — NOT OUR CONSCIOUSNESS IS COSMOCONSCIOUSNESS

LAST DAYS OF LEW WELCH

He ~~could feel~~ UNDERSTOOD ~~he~~ he was mortally
wounded — there was no way around it — he was good as
~~he was beginning~~ No
to get messages from the
other side — he switched
horizons — there was a way
out — when no one was looking
he slipped into the woods &
down a skid road — ~~at least~~
~~road~~ ~~nowhere~~ soon ~~he~~
he was at the end of the r~~oad~~
— then to the end of ~~the~~ the
last trail — it was X coun~~try~~
after that — at first he mo~~ved~~
fast as tho pursued with a
stride like Blake's trav~~eller~~
hasteth in the evening ~~f~~
~~wanted to disappear — he was~~
~~escaped by one creature~~
he work~~ed~~
his way down to the bottom of
a canyon & stepped ~~in~~
fast
into the ~~running~~ ~~the~~ water of
shallow creek over pocke~~ts~~
~~ran~~ thru fields of boulders ~~over~~
~~ways~~ ~~he stayed in the~~

COSMOVISION

THERE'S COSMOS OF CONSCIOUSNESS THAT ALL CREATION SHARES AS A COMMON — THE SUPPORT SYSTEM OF THE PHYSICAL UNIVERSE — REVIVE IDEA OF ETHER — CALL IT COSMOCONSCIOUSNESS — IT PERVADES UNIVERSE EVENLY IN ALL DIRECTIONS — OBJECTS DO NOT DISPLACE THIS ETHER OF COSMOCONSCIOUSNESS — THE ETHER PERVADES OBJECTS EVENLY AS EVENLY AS IT PERVADES SPACE BETWEEN OBJECTS — IT IS NOT HIGHER IN ONE THING OR CREATURE THAN IN ANOTHER — IT IS IN ALL EQUALLY — IT IS NO STRONGER INSIDE OUR HEAD THAN IT IS OUTSIDE OUR HEAD — IT EXPRESSES DIFFERENT IN EACH THING SO THERE ARE WORLDS & WORLDS — THERE ARE NEITHER HIGHER NOR LOWER WORLDS — THERE ARE MERELY DIFFERENT WORLDS — OUR BODYBRAIN IS A DEVICE FOR TRANSLATING COSMOCONSCIOUSNESS INTO EARTH TERMS — WE DO NOT ORIGINATE CONSCIOUSNESS WE TAP

INTO CONSCIOUSNESS — IT IS NOT OUR CONSCIOUSNESS IT IS COSMOCONSCIOUSNESS MANIFESTING THRU BODYMIND — THIS BODYMIND IS FOR HOMONID STYLE EARTH TRANSLATION OF COSMIC DESIRE — CARNATE IS DESIRE CARNATE — OUR BARE SELF CONSCIOUSNESS IS A DESIRE BODY — IT IS UNIVERSE WANTING SOMETHING — IT VISUALIZED US THEN PROJECTED US INTO THIS TIME LIKE SPACE — IT WANTED TO TRY US — I DONT THINK MOTHER UNIVERSE WILL BE REPEATING OUR STYLE TRIP ELSEWHERE — SHE SEES PLAINLY NOW WE WON'T DO — SHE SEES OUR TYPE DONT FIT IN — SHE'S KILLING US OFF — BUT THAT WAS IT — THE ORIGINAL HANGUP — WHEN WE BEGAN TO THINK WE ORIGINATE CONSCIOUSNESS — THAT OUR CONSCIOUSNESS ORIGINATES IN OUR BRAIN SO THAT NO BRAIN NO CONSCIOUSNESS — THAT INSIDE OUR BRAIN IS WHERE IT ALL STARTS — AND SINCE WE ORIGINATE CONSCIOUSNESS WE OWN IT & IF WE OWN IT WE CAN DO WHAT WE WANT WITH IT —

BUT CONSCIOUSNESS CANT BE BROKEN UP INTO INDIVIDUAL BITS EXCEPT IN PRIDE & IGNORANCE — A BIT OF CONSCIOUSNESS DONT WORK GOOD CUZ IT'S NOT WHOLLY CONNECTED — CONSCIOUSNESS DONT NEED BRAIN — BRAIN NEEDS CONSCIOUSNESS LIKE OUR BODY NEEDS AIR — WE PASS THRU COSMOCONSCIOUSNESS BREATHING IT IN & OUT OUR BRAIN — COSMOCONSCIOUSNESS DONT BELONG TO ANYONE SO IT CANT BE PERSONAL — THIS IS GOOD NEWS — IT MEANS WE NO LONGER HAVE TO LOAD OUR SHARE OF COSMOCONSCIOUSNESS SPOILED ONTO THIS IMPERSONAL PLENUM OF BEING THAT SHINES THRU US OF ITS OWN ACCORD WHETHER WE LIKE IT OR NOT WHETHER WE KNOW IT OR NOT — THIS ETHER OF INTELLIGENCE THAT CONTAINS THE IDEAL FORM OF EVERY POSSIBILITY & INVESTS EVERY PART OF UNIVERSE WITH ITS CHARACTER EQUALLY — SO WHY AM I LUGGING AROUND THIS EXCESS BAGGAGE OF SELFDOM OF DESIRE BODY GONE OUT OF WHACK WITH ITS OVERLARGE ANTLERS

EXTRAVAGANT PLUMAGE CUMBERSOME PELAGE THICK ARMOUR JUST FOR SKIN ITS MEGALOMANIC SIZE HUGE & OVERBEARING — YOU MEAN I CAN DROP IT LIKE A HOT POTATO — YOU MEAN I CAN DROP THIS OVERLONG EXERCISE IN SELF AUTHENTICATING CIRCULAR LOGIC SO I NO LONGER HAVE TO DO ITS ARITHMETIC WHERE THE SUM IS ALWAYS SUFFERING NO MATTER HOW I ADD IT UP — YOU MEAN I CAN SIMPLY EXCISE IT WHOLE & DROP IT INTO DUST BIN OF UNIVERSE — DROP IT — YOU'LL FEEL AS LIGHT & MINIMUM AS HUMAN CAN FEEL — YOU'LL BE NOTHING BUT COMPASSIONATE — THEN NO MORE SWEAT IN LIFE CUZ COMPASSION LIKE ULYSSES IS NEVER AT A LOSS — IN COSMOCONSCIOUSNESS WHAT WE CALL OURSELVES APPEARS WHOLLY UNNECESSARY & CHEAP JACK — LUCKILY IT'S DISPOSABLE

MAMA DID YOU CALL

I BELIEVE THAT AT A CERTAIN STAGE IN STAR SYSTEM FORMATION OUT OF MOTHER LIGHT THERE IS A RELEASE OF MYRIAD UNITS OF ZERO MASS PSYCHIC KNOTS INTO TIME LIKE SPACE — DESIRE BODIES — LET'S CALL THEM SOULS — LIKE ALL ENTITY SOUL IS AN IMPROBABLE STATE — PSYCHIC IMPROBABILITY IS A STRESSFUL STATE — SOUL ENDURES PAIN OF IMPROBABLE STATE — PUSHED THROUGH TIME LIKE SPACE BY STELLAR RADIATION IT SEEKS A VEHICLE AND A PLACE FOR EXPRESSING THIS PAIN IN A GRAPHIC MULTIDIMENSIONAL MANNER — POINT EARTH IN LOCAL UNIVERSE IS A STATION WHERE SOULS WHO SUFFER IN BROADLY SIMILAR WAYS CONGREGATE — SOULS MINERAL VEGETABLE & ANIMAL — EACH SOUL CALLING OUT ITS NAME IS WHAT WE COMPREHEND AS OUR EARTH WORLD — THE COURSE OF SOUL THROUGH BIRTHS & DEATHS IS CYCLIC WITH A WAVELIKE MOTION — BIRTH IS DEATH & DEATH IS BIRTH —

THEY ARE THE SAME AS PARTICLE & WAVE ARE THE SAME — EVERY SOUL KNOT WANTS TO UNRAVEL RELAX & DISAPPEAR FINALLY — AT THE SAME TIME EVERY ENTITY WANTS TO PERPETUATE ITS IDENTITY — HERE IS A RECIPE FOR SUFFERING — AT EACH PEAK & TROUGH OF SOUL'S WAVELIKE COURSE MOTHER LIGHT APPEARS & CALLS TO THE SOUL TO COME HOME NOW — BUT SOULS BECOME ENAMORED OF THEIR PAIN & DO NOT HEED THE CALL EVEN AS THEY HEAR IT — BUT EVERY SOUL FINALLY HEARS CLEARLY & GOES HOME & DISAPPEARS BACK INTO MOTHER LIGHT

DEVA WORLD

BEAUTIFUL WHILE IT LASTS BUT IT'S FOLLOWED BY A TIME WHEN BEAUTY FADES & SENSES FAIL TEETH FALL OUT BREATH BECOMES PUTRID & SKELETO-MUSCULAR SHRIVELS & STRIDE REDUCES TO SHUFFLE & FRIENDS AVOID YOU BECUZ YOU'RE NO LONGER AMUSING & YOU'RE DYING OR DEAD UNLESS YOU SOLVE OR YOUR LIFE RESOLVES FOR YOU RIDDLE OF IT HAS NO SIGHT NO TASTE NO SOUND NO TOUCH NO SMELL

SAME HORIZON DIFFERENT VIEW

BODHISATTVA OR ARHAT — NOW TOO MUCH BODHISATTVA NOT ENUFF ARHAT — BOTH IN SAME PLACE WITH SAME HORIZON BUT WITH DIFFERENT VIEW — BODHISATTVA LIKES HUMAN WORLD SO BLONDE HARD ROMANTIC THAT IS MISERICORDIA OUT OF EXQUISITE SUFFERING — THEY LIKE WHERE SUFFERING TURNS ANGELIC — THE EDGE OF SAME — BUT BODHISATTVA RIPE PERISHABLE MUST FALL TO GROUND AND EASY TO CORRUPTION — NO MATTER — BODHISATTVA LIKES TO GO AND COME BACK FOREVER & THAT'S A VOW — ARHAT SITS ON ROCK WITH UNIVERSE SQUEEZED BETWEEN THUMB AND FOREFINGER — A THIN TWIST OF SMOKE RISES FROM BETWEEN THUMB & FOREFINGER — NOT HUMAN — NOT ANIMAL — NO BINOMIAL — NO ADDRESS — NO TELEPHONE # — NO CREDIT — NO DEBIT — FAST AGAINST EVERY HOOK — IGNORANT — NOWHERE

TZADIKIM

I LIKE JUDAIC TZADIKIM — TZADIKIM IS ONE OF THE 36 PEOPLE IN EVERY GENERATION WHOSE EXISTENCE ON EARTH KEEPS THE WORLD FROM BEING ANNIHILATED — NOTHING CORPORATE ABOUT THIS GROUP — IT IS NOT A CLUB — IN FACT NONE OF THE 36 KNOWS OF THE EXISTENCE OF THE OTHERS — EACH IS ALONE — THEY DO NOT EVEN KNOW WHO THEY ARE OR WHAT THEY ARE DOING BUT BY THEIR RIGHTEOUSNESS THEY JUSTIFY THE CONTINUED EXISTENCE OF THE WORLD IN GOD'S EYE — WERE THEY NOT EACH IN THEIR PLACE DOING THEIR THING IN THEIR WAY THE WORLD WOULD BE DESTROYED AS AT THE TIME OF THE FLOOD

TO ROBERT AITKEN GYŌUN-KEN ROSHI ON HIS RETIREMENT PĀLOLO ZEN CENTER O'AHU HAWAI'I WINTER SOLSTICE 1996

COULD A SYNOPTIC OF IT RUN ALONG THESE LINES — COULD THE GIST OF IT BE THIS — OUT OF NOWHERE — A WARM LIGHT DROWNS YOU — & AS YOU DIE THERE'S THE THOT — OUT OF NOWHERE — NOTHING LEFT TO DO — & —ON THAT — COMPLETE RELEASE FROM EVERY BOND & YOKE — & — ON THAT — A RUSH OF QUIET GLORY TO EMPTY SILENT BLISS — IT COULD BE FOREVER — BUT THEN WACKO — RIGHT ON TOP OF THAT — THE THOT — OUT OF THE SAME NOWHERE — NECESSITY OF BODHISATTVA IDEAL — APPARENTLY YOU DO NOT GET THE ONE WITHOUT THE OTHER — THEY DON'T COME SEPARATE — THEY'RE LIKE YIN & YANG — FORM & EMPTINESS — THAT KIND OF ORIGINAL PAIR

— ARHAT & BODHISATTVA — YOU MUST TAKE THE SET OR NOTHING — SO — ON THE ONE HAND — YOU WANT TO KICK BACK AND RELAX NOW — NOW THAT YOU HAVE — NOTHING LEFT TO DO — & — YOU WANT NOTHING — WHILE ON THE OTHER HAND YOU GOT THE BODHISATTVA WORK ETHIC IDEAL — AN ETERNITY OF WORK — I SWEAR IN THIS WORLD YOU CAN'T WIN FOR LOSING

AGING
A DEPLORATION

IT HAPPENS SO SLOWLY THAT YOU CAN KEEP UP WITH IT AT FIRST WITH SUCCESSIVE MINOR ADJUSTMENTS OF ATTITUDE — BUT OVER THE LONG RUN THE CHANGE IS SO RADICAL THAT ONE DAY YOU SEE IT & YOU'RE SHOCKED FOR YOU CAN NO LONGER DENY IT — TO HAVE THE REMEMBRANCE OF WHAT WE WERE & HAVE TO SEE WHAT WE'VE BECOME — IT'S CRUEL — IF YOU WERE PUT TO THINKING UP A REFINED TORTURE FOR A MENTALITY SUCH AS OURS CARNATE LIKE US YOU WOULD THINK UP EXACTLY WHAT HAPPENS TO US — THE HARD PART IS THAT MENTALITY DOESN'T WANT TO ADJUST AS BODY BEGINS TO RUN DOWN — MENTALITY WANTS TO BE LIKE IT WAS IN LATE ADOLESCENCE WHEN FRESH BRAINBODY MADE WORLD FEEL FRESH & THATS HOW IT WANTS TO BE FOREVER WHICH WOULD BE GREAT BUT COMES AGING INTO ADULTHOOD OLD AGE DEATH — AGING IS EVEN

WORSE THAN DEATH — IT TAKES LONGER —
PRETTY IT HOW YOU WILL IT REMAINS OUR
HARDEST LESSON

I RESIGN

I RESIGN FROM THE EARTH & MOON — I RESIGN FROM THE SUN & ITS PLANETS — I RESIGN FROM THE STARS — I RESIGN FROM THE SKY — I RESIGN FROM BLUE — I RESIGN FROM NIGHT — I RESIGN FROM TIME AS WELL AS ETERNITY — I RESIGN FROM MEMORY — I RESIGN FROM SPACE & AIR — I RESIGN FROM OCEAN WITH WAVES — I RESIGN FROM WATER — I RESIGN FROM BOTH THE FLOWING RIVER & THE STILL LAKE — I RESIGN FROM RAIN — I RESIGN FROM CLOUD — I RESIGN FROM CLIMATE — I RESIGN FROM BRIGHT FLOWER & SWEET FRUIT — I RESIGN FROM THE TREE — EVEN THE APPLE TREE IN FULL FLOWER — I RESIGN FROM BEAUTY — I RESIGN FROM UGLY — I RESIGN FROM SEASHORE — MARINE TERRACE — HILL — VALLEY — PLAIN — DESERT — I RESIGN FROM EVERY MOUNTAIN — I RESIGN FROM HUMAN EXPECTATION — I RESIGN FROM DISEASE — I RESIGN FROM HEALTH — I RESIGN FROM ANIMAL — I RESIGN FROM FIRE WITH ITS

WARMTH & CHEER — I RESIGN FROM RACE CREED & COLOR — I RESIGN FROM MONEY & ENTERPRISE — I RESIGN FROM SCIENCE RELIGION HISTORY ART — I RESIGN FROM STATE — I RESIGN FROM CIVILIZATION — I RESIGN FROM OUR ERA — I RESIGN FROM ALL INFO DATA — I RESIGN FROM KNOWLEDGE — I RESIGN FROM IGNORANCE — I RESIGN FROM ENLIGHTENMENT — I RESIGN FROM SUFFERING — I RESIGN FROM THOT & FEELING — I RESIGN FROM INTERIOR VOICE — I RESIGN FROM SIGHT SOUND TASTE TOUCH & SMELL — I RESIGN FROM DESIRE SEX & ROMANCE — I RESIGN FROM EVERY WORLDLY COME ON — I RESIGN FROM SADNESS — I RESIGN FROM JOY — I RESIGN FROM NUCLEAR FAMILY OF MOM POP & KID SIBLINGS — I RESIGN FROM MYSELF — I RESIGN FROM HUMAN — I RESIGN FROM BODYMIND — I RESIGN FROM BIRTH LIFE & DEATH — I RESIGN FROM ALL BARDOS — THERE IS NOTHING LEFT TO DO — I AM DEAD — NO LONGER LOOK FOR ME

HAPPY ZEROETH BIRTHDAY

WAKE UP WITHOUT A SENSE OF AGE — MY PSI LIFE IN A NON ANNULAR MODE — RATHER THAN BEING AT SOME NUMERICAL POINT IN MY LIFE I AM IN MY LIFE AT A STILL POINT — I AM HERE — I AM OF NO AGE — I ONLY KNOW I WAS BORN & THAT I MUST DIE & THAT IN BETWEEN THERE IS A SUCCESSION OF REGULAR SOLAR LUNAR EARTH CYCLES THAT DO NOT ADD UP TO ANY KIND OF SUM — NO ARITHMETIC OF YEARS — O = O — I AM OF EACH SEASON — I AM SURPRISED WHEN THE SAME SEASON RETURNS

LAST DAYS OF LEW WELCH

*TO ANSWER YOUR QUESTION ABOUT LEW:
MANY BONES/SKULLS HAVE BEEN FOUND
BETWEEN MT TAMALPAIS & KITKITDIZZE IN THE
SIERRA FOOTHILLS WHERE HE DISAPPEARED &
THEY ARE ALWAYS COMPARED TO
LEW'S DENTAL X-RAYS & IT'S NEVER HIM.
SO NO PART OF HIS BODY WAS EVER FOUND.*
       MAGDA CREGG
       IN CORRESPONDENCE

HE UNDERSTOOD HE WAS MORTALLY WOUNDED — THERE WAS NO WAY AROUND IT — HE WAS GOOD AS DEAD — HE WAS BEGINNING TO GET MESSAGES FROM THE OTHER SIDE —HE SWITCHED HORIZONS — THERE WAS A WAY OUT — WHEN NO ONE WAS LOOKING HE SLIPPED INTO THE WOODS & DOWN A SKID ROAD — SOON HE WAS AT THE END OF THE ROAD — THEN TO THE END OF THE LAST TRAIL — IT WAS X COUNTRY AFTER THAT — AT FIRST HE MOVED FAST AS THO

PURSUED WITH A STRIDE LIKE BLAKE'S TRAVELER
HASTETH IN THE EVENING — HE WANTED TO
DISAPPEAR — HE WORKED HIS WAY DOWN TO
THE BOTTOM OF A CANYON & STEPPED INTO THE
FAST WATER OF ITS SHALLOW CREEK — IT RAN
THRU FIELDS OF BOULDERS & OVER POCKETS &
WAYS OF SAND — HE WALKED UPCREEK STAYING
IN THE WATER — THE CURRENT SLOWED HIM
DOWN — HE CAME TO A POOL DAMMED OFF BY
THE FOOT OF A SLOPE OF TALUS FALLEN FROM A
TOWERING FACE OF GREY GRANITE ABOVE — HE
TOOK OUT HIS PISTOL WITH SINGLE BULLET IN
CHAMBER — HE HELD THE PISTOL OUT OF WATER
& IMMERSED HIMSELF IN COLD MT POOL — WHILE
UNDERWATER IT CAME TO HIM GUN BRAIN BLAST
NOT THE WAY TO GO — HE CAME OUT OF THE
CREEK STEPPING FROM WATER TO ROCK — HE
STOOD AT THE BOTTOM OF THE TALUS SLOPE &
LOOKED UP AT THE ROCK FACE BEFORE HIM —
HIS FINAL PLACE WAS UP THERE — HE WANTED
A SPOT NO HUMAN HAD STOOD ON — A VIRGIN
SPOT — A PURE EARTH SPOT THAT DID NOT

BELONG TO ANYONE — THE ROCK FACE HAD HORIZONTAL FISSURES OF VARIOUS SIZES ACROSS IT FROM TOP TO BOTTOM LIKE NARROW STEPS — SOME HELD BENCHES WITH TREES GROWING ON EM — SOME FISSURES ENDED WITH CHUTES FILLED WITH EASY CLIMBING ROCKS — BETWEEN THE FISSURES UP THE FACE WERE LOTS OF MOVES & NO HARD EXPOSURE — SLOPE PERHAPS 40° — JUST HIS SPEED — HE WOULD CLIMB SLOW — HIS BODY WAS ON ITS LAST LEG — HE FOUND HIMSELF KNEELING TO ASK HIS BODY FOR THIS LAST FAVOR — THE LAST CLIMB TO THE LAST SPOT — HE WOULD ESCAPE THE UNDERTAKER & THE LEGAL WAY TO DIE — BEFORE STARTING HIS CLIMB HE LOOKED DOWN AT THE POOL & LISTENED TO THE MANY VOICES OF WATER RUNNING & POOLING — HE STARTED UP THE SLOPE OF TALUS — HALFWAY UP HE HEARD WATER TRICKLING FAR UNDER THE ROCKS — THE SOUND OF INVISIBLE WATER UNDER ROCKS TRICKLING TRICKLING CAUGHT HIM & MADE HIM PAUSE — IT WAS A SOUND FROM AN

UNDERGROUND WORLD HE COULD NOT SEE & IT SPOKE TO HIM OF DYING UNSEEN & ALONE — HE CONTINUED UPSLOPE — THE ROCK WAS HOT — THE SUN BEAT DOWN ON HIM — AT THE TOP OF THE TALUS SLOPE WHERE IT MET THE ROCK FACE WAS A NARROW BENCH WITH SOIL GRASS SHRUBS & TREES — HE FOUND A DIGGING STICK — HE BOWED TO THE STICK — HE KNELT & TOUCHED HIS HEAD TO THE GROUND — WITH NO THOT OR EFFORT ON HIS PART EVERY ACT BECAME FORMAL & IMPERSONAL — HE STARTED DIGGING OUT A SMALL HOLE — LOOSENING GROUND WITH STICK — REMOVING EARTH HANDFUL BY HANDFUL — HE WATCHED THE HOLE DEEPEN — WHEN THE HOLE WAS TO THE SIZE HE WANTED HE STOPPED — HE LOOKED INTO THE EMPTY HOLE — HE HAD DUG DOWN TO THE DEEPEST SECRET — IT WAS COMPLETE ABSOLUTION — HE HAD BEEN INNOCENT ALL ALONG — HE WEPT — HE LAID HIS PISTOL WITH BULLET IN HOLE — HE TOOK OUT HIS WALLET WITH ITS NOW LUGUBRIOUS CONTENTS & LAID IT IN THE HOLE

— HIS KNIFE FOLLOWED — THEN HIS NOTEBOOK & PENCIL — HE HAD WRITTEN HIS LAST WORD — HE KEPT HIS MATCHES — THEY WERE IN A SMALL WATERTIGHT FILM CAN — THAT WAS IT — NO MORE I D — NO MORE NUTHIN — JUST A DYING ANIMAL KNOWS IT'S DYING & WANTING TO DO IT IN SOLITUDE — HE COVERED THE HOLE & BRUSHED THE GROUND OVER IT — HE BRUSHED OUT HIS FOOTPRINTS & STEPPED ONTO THE ROCK FACE — HE LOOKED UP & PLOTTED HIS CLIMB — THERE WAS A LINE OF VEGETATION APPEARED & DISAPPEARED ALL THE WAY TO A NOTCH AT THE TOP — IT PROMISED WATER — THE WATER HE'D HEARD UNDER THE TALUS — HE WORKED OVER TOWARD IT — HE CLIMBED SLOWLY CONSERVING HIS STRENGTH — HE WANTED TO GET AS HIGH UP ON FACE AS HE COULD — THERE WOULD BE A PLACE — HE WOULD KNOW IT WHEN HE SAW IT — THE CLIMB TURNED OUT HARDER THAN HE'D THOT — ALL HANDS & FEET — HE BECAME ENGROSSED IN THE CLIMB — IT BECAME AN ACTIVE TRANCE STATE — HE FELT THE GOODNESS

OF ROCK AGAINST HIS BODY — EARTH FLESH — THE EXERTION THE SWEAT THE HEAT OF THE ROCK AGAINST HIS BODY GAVE HIM A HARDON — MOST ODD HE THOT AT THIS FUCKING EXTREMITY AFTER SO LONG AN ABSENCE — FUCK ROCK HE THOT — HE COULD FEEL THE CLIMB WAS TAKING HIS LAST STRENGTH — HE LAID HIMSELF FACE DOWN ON THE ROCK & FELT ENERGY FLOW INTO HIM — HE LOOKED DOWN THE WAY HE'D COME — THE CREEK WAS A THIN STRAND OF LIGHT THAT GLIMMERED & FLASHED AS IT MOVED DOWN CANYON — HE WAS HIGHER THAN HE'D THOT — HE LOOKED UP AND SAW A CHUTE LEADING TO THE TOP OF A NARROW FISSURE — HE CLIMBED TO THE TOP OF THE CHUTE & THERE BELOW HIM WAS A SMALL GRANITE FASTNESS WITH A BED OF CLEAN SAND — IT WAS A SHORT NARROW TROUGH WITH NO OUTLET — AN OPEN SARCOPHAGUS — THE PLACE — AT THE FAR END OF THE TROUGH WAS A MEAGER STAND OF STUNTED PONDO PINE & IN SOME GREEN ON THE FAR WALL HE SAW THE

GLINT OFF WATER RUNNING DOWN A RILL — WHERE THE RILL HIT THE GROUND THE WATER DIDN'T POOL BUT DISAPPEARED INTO ROCKS — HE MADE HIS WAY INTO THE TROUGH & LAID HIMSELF FACEDOWN ON THE HOT SAND — AT LAST — THERE WAS NO HURRY — NO URGENCY TO LIVE — NO PRIDE OF LIFE — HE COULD TRULY SAY HE WANTED IT — TO DIE — TO ADVANCE TO DEATH & EMBRACE DEATH AS HE WOULD A LOVER — THE HEAT OF THE SAND PENETRATED HIS BODY EASING THE PAIN & EXHAUSTION — HE FELT A WARM DULL SEX PANG IN LOINS LIKE A MEMORY OF SOMETHING THAT HAD HAPPENED IN ANOTHER TIME & COUNTRY — THERE AGAIN WAS UNCALLED FOR HARDON — HE GOT UP & WALKED TO THE RILL OF WATER — HE FELL TO THE RILL — PUSHING ASIDE THE MOSSES & SMALL FERNS HE PRESSED HIS MOUTH TO THE RUNNING WATER & DRANK DEEP — THEN HE RESTED HIS FACE ON THE WARM MOIST MOSS COVERED ROCKS AT THE BASE OF THE RILL — HE SMELLED DRIED PISS — RODENT PISS NO DOUBT — IT WAS

HOT — THE THOT OF CUNT SURFACED — HE CLOSED HIS EYES — IT WAS A HOT DAY & HE WAS RUNNING DOWN A PATH THRU A GRASSY FIELD — A CHILD RUNNING JUST TO BE RUNNING — HE FELT MOIST HOT & SWEATY — THEN A WARM HEAVY THRILL DEEP IN LOINS PULLED HIM TOWARD SOME UNKNOWN — HE FELL INTO THE GRASS BY THE SIDE OF THE PATH & HIS BODY WAS GRIPPED BY A RHYTHMIC PULLING TOWARD SOME MYSTERIOUS END — HE WENT FACEDOWN ON HOT GRASS & FUCKED THE GROUND TILL HE DISAPPEARED INTO A SPASM OF THRILL & THERE WAS A DAWNING AT THE TOP OF HIS SKULL — LIKE THEN NOW TOO NO SEMEN — THEN TOO EARLY NOW TOO LATE — PRONE THERE HE FELL ASLEEP — WHEN HE WOKE UP & TURNED OVER ON HIS BACK IT WAS LATE AFTERNOON WITH ITS SLANTING LIGHT — IT WAS STILL — THE SKY WAS CLEAR — HE HURT — THEN HE SAW THE SARCOPHAGUS WAS FILLED WITH THE GHOSTS OF HIS PASSING LIFE — HE STOOD UP TO QUESTION THEM BUT THEY DISAPPEARED AS THE ROCK

WALLS & THE GROUND HE STOOD ON BURST INTO
FLAME & SMALL MEMORY WORMS COVERED HIS
BODY & BURROWED INTO HIS SKIN TILL WITH A
SUPREME EFFORT HE BROKE OUT OF THE VISION
HOPPING & SCREAMING & CLAWING AT HIS SKIN
— HIS SCREAMS ECHOED AWAY ABSORBED BY
ROCK — HE WANTED REST — HE SAW WHERE A
FALLEN SNAG HAD BRIDGED OVER A DEPRESSION
IN THE GROUND — IT WAS CAVE SHELTER —
THERE WAS DRY DOWN WOOD ALL AROUND —
HE SMOOTHED THE SANDY SOIL INTO A BED &
LAY DOWN ON IT — HE TORE OFF A PLATE OF PINE
BARK FOR A PILLOW & LAID HIS HEAD ON IT —
NIGHT FELL — ROCK OF TROUGH HELD STILL
WARMTH WELL INTO NIGHT — WHEN IT GOT
COLD HE MADE SMALL FIRE & DOUSED IT BEFORE
LIGHT — DAYS PASSED — HE DIDN'T COUNT EM
— THEY PASSED IN AN EVEN PROCESSION — NO
MORE SECONDS MINUTES HOURS DAYS WEEKS
YEARS — THE QUAINTLY HUMAN PRISON OF TIME
— AS THE DAYS PASSED HIS INNER VOICE BEGAN
TO CUT OUT LIKE RADIO SIGNAL GETS WEAK

GOES DEAD — THEN THERE WAS THE SILENCE & THERE THE RECOGNITION — THE SILENCE THAT REQUIRED NOTHING — THE SILENCE THAT COULD IN NO WAY BE ADORNED — THE HURT FADED — ONE MORNING HE HEARD HIS NAME CALLED FROM ACROSS THE CANYON — HE GOT UP & LOOKED — HE SAW A GROUP OF SEARCHERS — HE KNEW THEM — THEY WERE BELOW CONTOURING ROUND A KNOLL BUSHWHACKING THRU CHAPARRAL — THEY WERE CALLING HIS NAME — HE OPENED HIS MOUTH & CURLED HIS TONGUE TO CALL BACK BUT NO VOICE CAME OUT — HE COULD NOT ANSWER — HE WAS NO LONGER THE ONE THEY WERE CALLING — LEW LEW LEW LEW LEW SOUNDED & DECAYED FROM SLOPE TO FARTHER SLOPE TILL THERE WAS UTTER RINGING SILENCE — TOWARD THE END HE MOVED OUT OF HIS SHELTER & LAY OUT ON THE OPEN GROUND WITH THE SKY ABOVE HIM — HE HAD FOUND THE PLACE WHERE NEITHER HEAT NOR COLD COULD REACH — HE WAS BEYOND HUNGER — HE WAS WAITING FOR ONE LAST

THING — IT CAME — ON THE LAST DAY TOWARD NOON HE SAW HIS VULTURE CIRCLE HIGH ABOVE HIM — IT HAD FOUND HIM — AFTER A LONG WHILE OF LAZY CIRCLING IT SLID DOWN THRU AIR TOWARD HIM WITH ITS STATELY ROCKING GLIDE & SWEPT OVER HIM COCKING ITS RED WATTLED HEAD WITH UNBLINKING EYE LOOKING DIRECTLY AT HIM — LEW LOOKED UP AND CAUGHT ITS EYE — THE PACT WAS MADE — THERE WAS NOTHING LEFT TO DO — HIS BREATHING BECAME SLOW & EASY THEN SLOWER & EASIER — EARTH TURNED INTO THE SHADOW OF NIGHT — THE STARS APPEARED WHEELING EVER WESTWARD — THERE WAS NO MOON — THEN FROM FAR BELOW DOWN CANYON HE HEARD THE FAINT HOOTING OF AN OWL & SOMETHING GAVE INSIDE HIM — HUSH FELL OVER HIS SARCOPHAGUS & AN EFFULGENCE OF WHITE LIGHT APPEARED STREAMING TOWARD HIM AS OUT OF A DOORWAY — THE LIGHT WAS QUIET & SUAVE WITH A SOFT CORUSCATION — A WOMAN APPEARED IN THE LIGHT — IT WAS

DOROTHY — SHE WAS SURPASSINGLY BEAUTIFUL — HER BREASTS WERE FILLED WITH MILK — SHE STEPPED FROM THE DOORWAY & CALLED INTO THE NIGHT COME HOME NOW — LEW ROSE UP WITH A HARDON HIS FACE BEAUTIFULLY EAGER & HE RAN TO THE LIGHT SHOUTING COMING MOTHER — HIS VOICE CRACKING WITH LOVE & DESIRE — SO EXCITED HE FORGOT TO BREATHE

ABOUT THE AUTHOR

PHOTO BY BOONE MORRISON

I WAS BORN FEB 4 1926 AT 8 AM IN LOS ANGELES — THE HOSPITAL I WAS BORN IN WAS EVENTUALLY TORN DOWN TO MAKE WAY FOR THE HOLLYWOOD FREEWAY SO NOW A JILLION CARS A DAY RUN OVER MY NATAL SPOT — YOU

CAN'T GET MORE AMERICAN THAN THAT — BOTH MY PARENTS HOWEVER WERE FROM JAPAN — AT THE TIME OF MY BIRTH MY FATHER WAS STUDYING TO BECOME A XTIAN PREACHER WITH THE EVANGELIST AIMEE SEMPLE MACPHERSON AT HER ANGELUS TEMPLE IN ECHO PARK — MY MOTHER WAS A JAPANESE SCHOOL TEACHER & WRITER — ONE OF MY EARLIEST MEMORIES IS OF GETTING UP PREDAWN & SEEING MY MOTHER ALREADY AT HER DESK SCRIBBLING SCRIBBLING — NOW I AM UP PREDAWN SCRIBBLING SCRIBBLING — MY CHILDHOOD WAS SPENT EAST OF LA IN THE SAN GABRIEL VALLEY WHICH WAS THEN RURAL & GIVEN OVER MOSTLY TO TRUCK FARMS & ORANGE & AVOCADO ORCHARDS — A THINLY POPULATED AREA — THIS FORMER RICH FARMLAND IS NOW TOTALLY HOUSED OVER & PACKED WITH PEEPS ALL UNDER A COVER OF THICK SMOG — A CIRCLE OF HELL DANTE MISSED — WITH ONSET OF WW II INNOCENCE OF CHILDHOOD & YOUTH BROKEN WHEN FDR THIS FORK TONGUED WASP TALKING DEMOCRACY

OUT OF ONE SIDE OF HIS MOUTH & RACIAL HATE OUT OF OTHER SIDE SIGNED HIS INFAMOUS EXEC ORDER 9066 DECREEING ALL JAPS CITIZEN & ALIEN ALIKE BE RIPPED OFF OF THEIR CONSTITUTIONAL RIGHTS & HOMES & BE CARTED OFF TO CONCENTRATION CAMPS IN REMOTE PARTS OF USA — OUR FAMILY WAS SENT TO A CAMP IN BIG HORN BASIN NW WYOMING — BEAUTIFUL BIG SKY COUNTRY HIGH PLATEAU SURROUNDED BY MTS — BEAUTIFUL EVEN FROM BEHIND BARBED WIRE FENCE WITH GUARD TOWERS ARMED GUARDS SEARCHLIGHTS ETC — I GRADUATED HIGH SCHOOL THERE — THEN I WAS DRAFTED INTO US ARMY — A SUPER CONTRADICTION BUT THERE WAS NUTHING ELSE HAPPENING AS FAR AS I COULD SEE SO I SPENT OVER 3 YRS IN ARMY SERVING IN US & ITALY IN AN ALL JAPANESE AMERICAN UNIT — FDR'S WAR TO SAVE DEMOCRACY FOUGHT WITH A RACIALLY SEGREGATED ARMY — FDR STALIN CHURCHILL VS HITLER TOJO MUSSOLINI — WHATTA CREW — WHATTA MATCHUP — WHATTA LAUGH IF YOU

SURVIVED — WHILE IN THE ARMY I BECAME INTERESTED IN LITERATURE — IT WAS READING HEMINGWAY'S A FAREWELL TO ARMS THE BEAUTIFUL OPENING SENTENCES OF THIS BOOK THAT DID IT — I REMEMBER THINKING NOW THIS IS BEAUTIFUL THIS MUST BE WHAT'S CALLED LITERATURE — THIS CARE FOR WORDS — AFTER ARMY A SHORT STINT IN NYC THEN DENVER THEN DRIFTED BACK TO LA — HERE IN THE LATE '40S A CHANCE MEETING INTRODUCED ME TO THE ZEN MONK NYOGEN SENZAKI THE PIONEER TEACHER OF ZEN IN ENGLISH ON THE WEST COAST — I WILL BE FOREVER GRATEFUL TO THIS MAN FOR OPENING THE QUESTION OF THE GREAT MATTER TO ME — I ALSO MANAGED 5 YRS AT USC DURING SAME TIME — I MAJORED IN INTERNATIONAL POLITICS WITH MINOR IN CHINESE — I HAD TAKEN UP THE MAJOR BECUZ OF A VAGUE ROMANTIC IDEA I WANTED TO TAKE AFTER THE GREAT FRENCH DIPLOMAT POETS PAUL CLAUDEL & ST JOHN PERSE — THE SYSTEM SOON DISABUSED ME OF THIS IDEA — MY

MASTERS THESIS WAS ABOUT WHY & HOW VIETNAM WAS PARTITIONED IN TWO AFTER WW II — I NEVER FINISHED THE THESIS AS ABOUT THEN I DECIDED INTERNATIONAL POLITICS WAS NOT A SUBJECT I WAS TRULY INTERESTED IN — I DROPPED OUT IN THE LATE '50S & MOVED TO SF AS LA BEGAN TO SMOG OUT BAD — IN SF BY ANOTHER LUCKY CHANCE I MET THE VERY CHARISMATIC DAVID HUNTER A PIONEER TEACHER IN WHAT LATER CAME TO BE KNOWN AS THE HUMAN POTENTIAL MOVEMENT — THRU HIS GROUP I MET MANY PEOPLE KNOWN AS THE BEATS — I LIVED THEN IN CHINATOWN NEXT TO NORTH BEACH WHERE THE BEAT MOVEMENT WAS HAPPENING — THIS WAS A TIME OF EXPANDING HORIZONS FOR ME — THIS WHOLE TIME WAS SUMMED UP FOR ME IN A CRAZY CROSSCOUNTRY DRIVE I TOOK WITH JACK KEROUAC & LEW WELCH THAT ENDED UP IN LOWER EASTSIDE APT OF ALLEN GINSBERG — THIS TRIP IS DESCRIBED IN A KEROUAC WELCH SAIJO COLLABORATION ENTITLED TRIP TRAP — I'M

ALSO ONE OF THE HUNDREDS OF REAL PEOPLE JACK GOT INTO HIS NOVELS — I'M IN BIG SUR — HERE ALSO BEGAN MY EXPERIENCE WITH CERTAIN KEY PLANTS LIKE MARIJUANA & PEYOTE — MY FIRST PEYOTE TRIP IN LATE '50S WHEN TIME MELTED LIKE A DALI WATCH HOOKED ME ON PARANORMAL SPACE FOREVER — AROUND 1960 I MOVED FROM SF ACROSS THE GOLDEN GATE BRIDGE TO MARIN COUNTY TO THE VILLAGE OF MILL VALLEY WHERE I BOUGHT A HOUSE ON THE SIDE OF MT TAMALPAIS THE PRESIDING EMINENCE OF THE AREA — I SPENT PRETTY MUCH OF THE NEXT 20 YRS IN MARIN ENDING UP ON INVERNESS RIDGE OVERLOOKING TOMALES BAY IN WEST MARIN — DURING THE '60S & '70S I WAS YOUR BASIC MARIN COUNTY HIPPIE STONER — LONG HAIR LOOSE CLOTHES FREE LIVING & ON THE FLOOR CUZ CHAIRS SEEMED A FORM OF REPRESSION — WE USED TO BELIEVE THERE WERE MORE STONERS PER CAPITA IN MARIN THAN ANYWHERE ELSE IN THE WORLD — I SPENT MOST OF THE '60S STONED ON ACID PEYOTE

MUSHROOMS & OF COURSE MARIJUANA THIS MOST SACRED PLANT THAT HAS STOOD H. SAPIEN IN GOOD STEAD FOR MILLENNIA IN SPITE OF THEIR PROFOUND SAPPINESS — DURING THIS TIME I BECAME INTERESTED IN FASTING ON WATER AS A WAY TO GET HIGH & ENDED UP DOING MY BIBLICAL 40 OR IN MY CASE 45 DAY FAST WHICH GAVE ME AN UTTERLY TRANSFORMING EXPERIENCE — I ALSO MANAGED TO SQUEEZE IN A MARRIAGE ROUNDABOUT HERE THAT FAILED SADLY THO IT WAS FULL OF INSTRUCTION — I SPENT A LOT OF TIME IN THE HIGH SIERRA WHICH WAS A SAVING GRACE FOR ME IN THOSE DAYS — I EVEN WROTE A PRIMER ON BACKPACKING ENTITLED BACKPACKER NOW OUT OF PRINT — I CONSIDER MYSELF A CHILD OF THE '60S — IT WAS WHEN I BECAME A REBORN HUMAN — WHAT THOSE TIMES SHOWED ME WAS THE INFINITE RANGE OF THE HUMAN IMAGINATION WITHIN INFINITE OVERMIND — BY THE END OF THE '60S INTO THE '70S ALL MY CIRCLE HAD BEEN HIGH SO MANY TIMES WE HAD COME DOWN SO

MANY TIMES — & EACH TIME WE CAME DOWN WHO WE WERE LOST MORE CREDIT COMPARED TO WHERE WE'D BEEN WHICH SHOOK US UP — WHO AM I & WHAT IS THIS I DOING — MARRIAGES FAILED FRIENDSHIPS BROKE UP — EVERYONE WANTED TO BE DIFFERENT THAN WHO THEY WERE — OUR MARIN HAD BECOME A ZOO — THE CALL WAS HEAD FOR THE BOONIES — THE '60S HAD BEEN SUPER GREGARIOUS NOW WE WANTED SOLITUDE MORE SPACE MORE PRIMITIVE SPACE OR WE WANTED AN EXCLUSIVE COMMUNITY OF LIKE MINDED — PEOPLE BEGAN TO DISAPPEAR INTO SONOMA MENDOCINO HUMBOLDT & TRINITY COUNTIES — YOU HEARD OF COMMUNES — MEANTIME I HAD MARRIED AGAIN — SHE WAS A TEACHER FROM SONOMA & A MUSICIAN IN A ROCK & ROLL BAND THAT PLAYED CLUBS IN MARIN SONOMA & MENDOCINO — THIS SECOND MARRIAGE HAS LASTED — IT HAS BEEN TO THE MILTONIC STANDARD FOR A COMPANIONATE MARRIAGE — AMOROUS & RELAXING FULL OF PLEASING CONVERSATION CHEER COMFORT

COMPATIBILITY & THE GENIAL BED — WE MOVED TO SOME UNIMPROVED LAND IN HUMBOLDT COUNTY — TO THE LOST COAST SO NAMED FOR ITS REMOTENESS AT FAR WESTERN EDGE OF CONTINENT — WE BECAME LOCAL PRIMITIVES — HOMESTEADING AN UNIMPROVED PIECE OF LAND WILL DO THAT TO YOU — YOU LEARN BASICS LIKE WHERE DOES YOUR WATER COME FROM & DOES YOUR PLACE HAVE AN ALL SEASONS ACCESS ROAD — YOU CLEAR SOME LAND BUILD SHELTER PUT IN GARDENS — THE LIFE HERE WAS INTENSE ENDLESSLY INTERESTING EVEN EXHILARATING BUT THINGS SPOIL FAST IN AMERICA — STILL WE HAD 12 GOOD YEARS THERE — THAT'S PRETTY GOOD FOR NOWADAYS — THEN BY AN ODD LEGERDEMAIN OF FATE WE ARE TRANSPORTED TO A SMALL CLEARING IN AN UPLAND 'ŌHI'A LEHUA HĀPU'U FOREST AT 4000' EDGING AN ACTIVE VOLCANO — ANOTHER EDGE — LIKE THEY SAY IF YER NOT LIVIN ON THE EDGE YER TAKIN UP TOO MUCH SPACE